Pip and Zoe's
Amazing Adventures

Zoe Cottew

Emmie
PRESS

First published in 2024 by Emmie Press, an imprint of Notebook Group Limited, 11 Arden House, Deepdale Business Park, Bakewell, Derbyshire, DE45 1GT.

www.notebookpublishing.com
ISBN: 9781913206062

A CIP catalogue record for this book is available from the British Library.

Typeset by Emmie Press of Notebook Group Limited

A lovingly written collection of exotic childhood adventures. Zoe's stories are so vivid I felt like I had actually lived them myself.

— ADAM HILLS
Comedian and Radio and Television Presenter

A beautifully realised love letter to an idyllic upbringing, complete with stunningly evocative illustrations. Everyone should be gifted a childhood like Zoe's. Share this instant classic with your kids.

— STEPHEN CURRY
Actor, Writer, and Fishing Enthusiast

Amazing adventures indeed as the world, and especially the natural world, unfolds before Pip and Zoe. It's so important to be curious, and their curiosity is rewarded in some extraordinary settings.

— JIM DARBY
Author and Journalist
(*The Age* and *The Sydney Morning Herald*)

THOUSAND ISLAND
DREAMING

Chapter One

'*Wheee*!' squealed Zoe as Pip whooped.

It was glorious. Clinging to the grab rails, their feet dangling over the bow of the boat and the sea whooshing away underneath, it felt like they were flying. The weather was *perfect*. The sky stretched blue and clear to the horizon, and the sunshine reflected brilliantly off the cerulean waves, like fallen stars flashing on the surface. The swell was smooth and rolling, and at the peak of the swell and with the bow pointed to the endless sky, they felt like the sea eagles soaring above.

The twins, Pip and Zoe, shrieked with joy as

the twin hulls of the powered catamaran splashed into the trough, drenching them with salt spray and happiness.

Everyone was smiling. Diana, Ben, Mandy, and Sam (Pip and Zoe's cousins) were all positioned at a post around the bow, soaking wet and laughing. Margie, their mother, meanwhile, sat contentedly with their father Charles' arm around her as they both leaned against the cabin window. Zoe noticed that even the captain looked happy, grinning and joking at the helm with his first mate as they navigated the swell.

Crossing the deep shipping channel of the Java Sea to get to the Thousand Islands could be treacherous, so it was always a good day when the seas chose to be kind.

Before long, the swell gave way to the calm blue shallows of the reefs around the islands. The brown polluted water that slopped around the rickety piers at the port of Ancol Marina, North Jakarta, was far behind them. It was as though there was a magical veil they had passed through the moment they'd crossed the shipping channel, leaving behind the industry and smoke of tankers, ships, and cargo boats, and had sailed into the magical, vibrant world of small green islands and dazzling blue water. Zoe loved the shifting colours of the water; how it glimmered from dark blue to azure to pale blue as the corals gave way to sand.

'Which island are we staying on?' Pip asked excitedly.

Pointing to the second island from the left, Charles announced, 'Papa Theo!'

Bumping alongside the pier against the makeshift fenders (which were made of old tyres and decommissioned buoys), shouts were made, ropes were thrown, cleat hitch knots were tied around the hitches, and loops were secured around the cleat horns. A final clove knot was also pulled tight around a piling, just to be sure.

Finally, the boat engine was stilled. The sound of the wind, birds, and water slapping against the pylons filled their ears. A collective relief se-

-emed to settle on them all.

They had arrived.

At last, the metal gangplank was lowered so the passengers could carefully step off the port side of the boat and onto the creaking timber planks of the pier. Chattering and pointing with delight at the fish crowding the pylons, the children could hardly wait to step onto the gangplank, unconsciously jostling each other and those around them.

'This is the longest pier I've ever seen!' Sam exclaimed. The pier stretched from the outer rim of the reef that encircled the island and over the inviting blue lagoon before disappearing into the shade of the casuarina trees, where they could see a glimpse of the cottages beyond.

Margie cautioned the impatient children. 'Remember to be polite, show respect, and calm down. There will be plenty of time to explore.'

'Yes, yes!' The children's heads bobbed in a disorderly collective of nodding. They were only half listening, swept up as they were in their anticipation.

After being greeted by the island staff, the passengers took turns bowing their heads in return for the fragrant frangipani leis. They took the green coconuts, pink straws jauntily poking out, that were handed to them.

As she walked the length of the pier, pointing at every shadow and flitting fish, Zoe couldn't wait to pass the coconut to someone else. She had dutifully thanked the woman who had given it to her and pretended to drink, but the truth was, the smell of coconut water made her gag: she had once drunk one that had been mixed with coloured palm sugar and it had given her a dreadful case of gastro. Ever since then, she hadn't been able to stomach the stuff.

Quickly glancing around, Zoe gently put the coconut on a low bamboo table in the reception pavilion as they all gathered to check in and collect the keys to their cottages. They watched as the boat was unloaded of its supplies along with their luggage and fishing rods. Everything was being piled precariously high on the trolleys that were being pulled up and down the pier, pitching and jolting over the uneven sleepers.

Finally, they had their keys, so they made their way along the tidily swept sand pathways lined with crotons and the occasional garden lantern. The paths were swept daily, but not often enough to protect their bare feet from the painful stab of the constantly falling casuarina seed cones! The casual plantings of casuarina trees and coconut palms gave the pathways a lovely, dappled shade, and the white sand shone brilliantly just beyond. At night, when the winds came in, the casuarinas provided the whisperings of woodwind to the clatter and percussion of the palm fronds. Interrupted by the distant *ting-ting-ting* of the flag clips against the one flagpole at the end of the pier, it was a nightly tropical orchestra.

The red-and-white Indonesian flag was perpetually raised, faded and tattered from exposure.

'Right, kids!' Margie called, clapping her hands to get the children's attention. 'Boys are in Cottage Three, Charles and I are in Cottage Two, and you girls are in Cottage One.'

She handed out the keys, which were attached to large rectangles of wood with the relevant cottage number hand-carved on both sides. The boys elbowed each other out of the way, grasping for their key, since they knew whoever got it would open the cottage first. Meanwhile, the girls acquiesced calmly to Diana being handed the key. She was the eldest by two years, so she naturally took the leadership position.

With the keys in their possession, the children all stood, awaiting further instruction. Margie looked at them expectantly and then said, 'Right, well then, off you go! Have fun.'

In a sudden spark of activity, the boys scampered to their cottage (the one that was furthest away) and the girls turned down the pathway that led to theirs. With their low, thatched, gabled rooves, whitewashed walls made of coral and cement, and small timber-framed casement windows, the cottages were charming.

After fumbling with the heavy lock and key, Diana pushed the door open. It swung inwards against the wall to the left. The cottage only had one simple room, which was filled with beds. There was one door to enter (the one Diana had just opened) and one door at the far end, which opened onto an outdoor bathroom.

Zoe got the bed by the front door. She threw herself onto it and leaned against the pillows, thrilled that they had the cottage with the best feature of all: the wall that she faced had been built around an enormous fish tank. It was like a living painting that lit up the gloom of the cottage. Tropical fish swam about the coral, and shells peppered the sandy bottom. Going to sleep at night with their faces bathed in pale blue light, listening to the burble of the pump and watching the fish swim, was heaven to the children.

After settling in, the children spent the afternoon reacquainting themselves with the island, swimming in the lagoon, readying their fishing equipment, and planning the days ahead. Before supper, everyone gathered on the sand, overlooking the pier and the lagoon. The adults sat on bamboo recliners, which had been pulled into a haphazard circle, and the children perched on the ends of the chairs or sat on the sand. Ice clinked in drinks. The children revelled in the treat of having 7Up. The sun had lowered into the horizon, softening the bleached light of the day into a kaleidoscope of pastels — pinks, oranges, and blues — while the sea lost its brilliance and faded into moody greys and greens.

It was peaceful, and the mood was calm. Pip and Zoe were quietly drawing pictures in the sand with twigs and listening to their father, Charles, recount some history of the area.

'Onrust Island was claimed and developed by the Dutch in the seventeenth century. It was a crucial stop for ships coming to and from Indonesia during the spice trade and wars. Even Captain Cook's *HMB Endeavour* stopped at the island in 1770 for repairs after it had run aground on the Great Barrier Reef off Queensland,' explained Charles. 'It has also been used as prison and a quarantine centre. It was a leprosarium at one stage, as well.'

'What's a leprosarium?' asked Pip curiously.

'A place where people with leprosy were put to stop it from spreading in the community.'

Zoe thought of the beggars she had seen in Jakarta with inflamed lesions and sores all over their arms and legs, and felt sorry. She struggled to understand why it had to be that wealth and poverty lived side by side. She thought of the beggar she had seen reflected in the shiny glass windows of the high rises along Jalan Sudirman. The view from the high-rise shopping malls would always draw her eyes not to the horizon, but to the slums built in jostled space around their perimeters. This bothered Zoe, as did the fact that what circumstances you were born into seemed entirely down to chance.

Standing and shaking off the sand, Zoe

slipped her hand into her father's as they all walked barefoot to the restaurant for supper.

Once they were full and bored of conversation, the children asked to be excused. Pip had noticed the fishermen casting off the end of the pier for squid, and wanted to join them. Diana and Mandy weren't quite so interested in fishing, however, so they went back to the cottage to relax. Zoe, on the other hand, joined the boys to see what the fishermen had brought in.

The wind had picked up and tugged at Zoe's sarong as they walked along the pier, careful not to trip on the uneven sleepers or to impale their toes with another vicious splinter. A spotlight tethered to the flagpole cast a bright white circle of light onto the water, the edges constantly shifting with the lift and tumult of wavelets that were being stirred up by the wind. Ghostly white shapes darted about near the water's surface.

'Did you know that the squid are activating their counter illumination camouflage against the spotlight and can match their colours to their surroundings to camouflage themselves?' mused Pip, to no one in particular. 'I think they have things called chromatophores in their skin that make them able to do it. Their skin also has light reflectors called iridophores and leucophores that, when activated, create changeable skin patters of polarized light in milliseconds.'

Ben, Sam, and Zoe stared at Pip. He didn't say much, but when he did, he came out with extraordinary statements with words no one else could pronounce, never mind understand.

'How do you *know* that?' Sam asked.

'Dunno,' Pip shrugged, keeping his eyes on the darting squid.

Ben, Sam, and Zoe exchanged looks, eyebrows raised and incredulity widening their eyes.

Sitting down at the edge of the pier with their legs dangling over, the children watched the fishermen cast their lines and lures into the dark water time and time again. They noticed that the fishing line was wound around old soft drink cans and that the fishermen kept the lures shallow and skimmed them across the water, winding up the line rapidly before casting again. Every now and then, a squid would dart though the water to catch its perceived prey, only to snag its mouth on the sharp hooks.

As the fisherman hauled the squids onto the pier, their tentacles writhed and wrapped around the lure and line in panic. Ink would spray and their bodies would make a splat on the dry wood, and then, suddenly, they'd be dead, after being swiftly cut in half by the fisherman's knife.

'And that's what you call calamari,' Ben said flatly.

Tired of watching the frantic casting and reeling, the children bade the fishermen goodnight and made their way slowly back to their cottages. They had another day of adventure ahead of them.

Chapter Two

Zoe awoke to the dawn light seeping in through the window. Mandy and Diana were still fast asleep. Creeping to the bathroom, Zoe put her bathers on, which were still damp from the day before. Shivering slightly, she added a T-shirt to stave off the coolness that still lingered from the night.

Tiptoeing past the girls, Zoe slipped out through the front door and collected her rod and some leftover bait from the day before, which looked and smelled terrible.

It had rained recently, and the sand was flattened and pockmarked. Zoe could feel the ridges of each pock under her feet, the sand cool and damp. It was a nice feeling seeing her feet make the first marks of the day.

As Zoe settled at the end of the pier, she noticed that the morning was overcast and grey. The water was clear but bereft of its brilliant midday blue. What's more, there was no sign of any squid darting around in the water. The only evidence that last night's frenzy had ever taken place was the black splotches of ink that stained the timber planks. Zoe wondered if they would fade with time.

Zoe half-heartedly cast her rod and waited. The wind had dropped, and the world felt sleepy and quiet. She watched the shifting light of dawn in a daze.

Sometime later, the first ray of morning light cast golden and warm across the water, making her squint. She realized she was starving. She reeled in the line and threw the rest of the bait into the sea and, wandering over to the restaurant, found that her parents were already there, black coffee steaming and eggs and bacon half-eaten. They both looked tanned, relaxed, and happy.

'Good morning, darling,' said Charles, smiling over his coffee. Zoe leaned against him for a cuddle. 'What is that *smell*?' His face contorted into a disgusted expression.

Grinning, Zoe held up her hands. 'Bait.'

'Go and wash up,' ordered Margie, a look of consternation creasing her brow.

Clean but not completely rid of the dead bait smell, Zoe settled back at the table for breakfast.

'What's on the agenda for today?' asked Charles.

'Um, maybe some fishing from the canoes?' mumbled Zoe through a mouthful of buttery toast.

'Sounds lovely. Just make sure you let us know what you're up to,' Margie said.

Zoe nodded in reply. Little did she know that it was a promise they would all break.

*

Wading in the shallows near the pylons of the pier as she waited for the others to finish breakfast and start the day, Zoe saw a tiny octopus puffing along. She gently scooped it up with her net and put it in her bucket (both of which she *always* seemed to have at hand.) Marvelling at the little creature, which was light and sandy in colour with tiny dark dots all over its skin, she thought its large dark eyes seemed to be staring right back at her as its tentacles furled and unfurled around its body. Gently dipping her hand in the bucket and cupping it under the octopus, she lifted it out of the water to get a closer look. It barely filled her palm.

As she brought it closer to her face, she could feel the suction cups on its tentacles sticking to her skin. Zoe was peering at the beautiful creature more closely when she was suddenly squirted with ink. It jetted out and sprayed an arc of dark blue across the front of her T-shirt, startling her.

'What've you got?' Pip asked as he waded up to her, Sam and Ben trailing behind.

'A baby octopus,' Zoe said with excitement, lifting her hand to show the boys.

'It inked you!' laughed Sam, pointing.

'I know! Impressive for such a little thing.'

'You know, everyone calls them tentacles, but they're actually called arms,' said Pip knowingly, pointing at the little ten... *arms* curling around Zoe's fingers.

'We should call you Dr Doolittle,' teased Ben, giving Pip a light elbow in the ribs. Pip flinched and grinned. To him, there wasn't a better compliment in the world.

After they had all finished peering at the octopus and admiring its perfection, Zoe released it into the clear blue water. They watched it billow its arms and then suddenly squeeze them together, straight as an arrow, and dart away.

They spent the rest of the morning happily canoeing, fishing, and swimming, ravenously devouring their fried rice and noodles at lunchtime. It had been a happy morning indeed.

*

'Your turn!' declared Diana. They were all playing Uno, sitting in the sand and shaded by the casuarina trees. They were using a low bamboo table to lay the cards out, but because of the sloping sand, the cards kept sliding to the edge, making it easier to cheat.

Pip, having lost interest long ago, was leaning back on his elbows and contemplating the view. 'We should swim to Pulau Putri,' he said matter-of-factly.

All the children turned to look at the island opposite. It seemed to be just beyond the end of the pier.

'It looks deep between the islands,' Sam pointed out, furrowing his brow in concern.

'What about the barracuda we saw today?' added Zoe.

'Barracuda don't eat people,' Pip replied, his gaze still fixed on Pulau Putri.

This didn't do much to reassure Zoe, who recalled the vicious-looking teeth, overshot bottom jaw, and long, silvery-blue body with what looked like tiger stripes.

'How far do you think it is?' asked Diana.

This was met with shrugs and 'dunno's.

'It doesn't look *that* far,' Mandy said, with bravado.

'Shall we do it?' Diana asked excitedly.

Nervous, Sam and Zoe objected. 'I don't think it's a good idea,' Sam insisted.

'What happens if we don't make it?' added Zoe.

'We'll make it,' Pip said firmly, getting up and grabbing his fins.

Glancing nervously at each other, the children stood, dusted off the sand, and set about gathering their fins. They accepted that this challenge was now inevitable.

'Aim for the left of the island,' instructed Pip as they waded into the water. 'The current looks like it's washing towards the right. If we aim left, we should end up somewhere in the middle.'

Looking worried, Sam and Zoe glanced at

each other as they rinsed the sand out of their fins. They wiggled their feet into the stiff and sticky rubber as Pip and Diana started to swim out.

'Wait for me!' Zoe pled as she struggled to get her fins on.

'We need to stay together,' Mandy added.

Once everyone was ready, the group swam over the rim of the reef and into the deep blue water. They all kept as close to Pip and Diana as possible. They were all swimming sidestroke, on their backs, or freestyle with their heads up, making sure to keep each other in sight. It didn't take long for the giggles and excitement to give way to puffing and fatigue.

'Maybe we should turn back?' Sam said breathlessly after a while.

'I think we're almost halfway,' Pip said dismissively. 'Keep going.'

Zoe looked back. The island they had left looked as far away as the island they were swimming to. The water was dark, and it suddenly felt menacing. Turning back didn't feel like much of an option, but neither did pressing on.

What choice did they have now that they were in the middle of the ocean?

Rolling onto her back, Zoe focused on the white clouds in the sky. Kicking her legs rhythmically, she drew deep, regular breaths to try and control her anxiety. Glancing at each other from time to time, Zoe could tell that they were all questioning whether this had been a good idea at all.

But they kept swimming. There was no spare breath or energy for talking.

After what felt like an age, Diana exclaimed, 'The water's changing colour!'

Rolling over, Zoe could see the deep blue had, indeed, faded to a lighter blue, and she felt a rush of relief. It meant that the water was becoming shallower. Looking up, she realised the island now looked close. It was within reach!

Encouraged, the children changed to freestyle, and the outlines of the coral started to appear out of the blue. As they swam, more details could be seen in the water, including fish, coral, and sand. As they approached the coral rim, they were careful not to knock the black sea urchins and spike themselves on their sharp, poisonous spines.

As quickly as the water had turned deep blue when they'd started, the water suddenly turned clear and light as the sun reflected off the white, sandy bottom of the lagoon.

Elated and grinning but far too tired for whoops, the children drifted into the shallows and flopped onto the sand, breathing raggedly.

'We made it,' Mandy breathed.

Closing her eyes, Zoe lay down on the sand, with relief. They all lay still for some time. Then, quite suddenly, Pip announced, 'Right. Let's explore!'

Groaning, the children sat up, picked up their fins, and traipsed up the sand to explore the island.

'The resort looks closed,' Sam said slowly, echoing everyone else's thoughts.

'Hope not,' Pip said, pulling a little plastic

container from his shorts, where he kept his money. 'I need a 7Up.'

'You'd better have enough money for all of us!' Diana shrieked.

'Not my fault you didn't think of it,' retorted Pip with a grin.

Diana punched him playfully on the arm. They all suddenly realized how thirsty they were.

'There's someone!' declared Ben, pointing.

Waving, the children greeted the approaching Indonesian woman, who smiled at them. *'Kalian tiba disini dari mana?'* she asked. (Where did you come from?)

'Kami berenang dari Papa Theo,' explained Pip. (We swam from Papa Theo.)

'Wah astaga! Kalian gila!' (My goodness! You're crazy!)

Laughing but feeling a little sheepish, the children asked if the reception was open. They needed to buy some drinks.

'Iya, ayo,' the woman nodded, beckoning them to follow her.

Minutes later, the children were sitting in bamboo chairs and sharing the three 7Ups that they could afford. As soon as they all took a sip, they almost instantly felt better and more energised.

After wandering around for a while, exploring the island, Diana said, 'You know we have to swim back, right?'

'Yeah, we should probably get going. We don't want it to get dark while we're in the water,' Ben shrugged.

Suddenly nervous, Zoe agreed, 'We need to start now!'

As they made their way back to where they'd washed up, they all silently thought that it suddenly seemed quite late in the day. No one was wearing a watch, so they couldn't be quite sure what time it was, but it certainly seemed later than they'd have liked. Wasting no time in rinsing and fitting their fins, the children started to swim. It was surprising to them how the light water of the lagoon gave way to the deep blue more quickly than before.

The children had a more anxious sense of purpose this time. There was no time to dither or talk. Despite their adrenaline, it felt like fatigue was setting in almost immediately, but they had to keep going.

As she swam, Zoe noticed uneasily that the sun was slipping closer to the horizon. She hated the shadows the late afternoon sun cast in the water. It gave her the creeps.

As she kept going, her legs ached. Badly.

'Keep going,' puffed Diana, sensing that everyone was flagging. As the eldest, she felt it was her responsibility to encourage everyone. This inspired her to dig deep and be strong, although she was admittedly starting to feel scared, too.

'It feels like there's a current,' said Ben. 'It doesn't feel like we're moving…'

'Yep, I agree. I think we're swimming into it,' Pip gasped. 'The last thing we want is to end up in Singapore, or to get swept through the Sunda Strait and out into the Indian Ocean!'

He was trying to make everyone smile, but

Zoe started to cry.

'Don't waste your energy on crying, Zoe,' Mandy instructed sternly. 'You'll need it to swim! C'mon, you can do it!'

Trying to hold her tears back, Zoe nodded.

'Let's all do twenty strokes of freestyle, faces down, and then check in and rest. Then, we'll do it again,' Pip suggested.

Zoe thought this was a clever thing to do. It would make them all focus on counting rather than letting the fear take hold.

They all took twenty strokes and then stopped, counted each other, and kicked for a while to catch their breath.

'Ready? Let's do it again,' Pip commanded.

Heads down and legs kicking, they all counted twenty strokes, stopped, checked in, and again caught their breath. They did this over and over for what felt like forever. All the while, the sun kept slipping lower and lower towards the horizon, and the children realized with dismay that the island still didn't seem to be getting any closer.

'One, two, three, four, five, six...' Zoe counted, breathing bilaterally. *It's so lucky that we're all strong swimmers*, she thought. For the first time, she was very grateful that their mother had made them train in the pool every week. Margie had been a state swimming champion back in Australia, and her grandmother in England had had aspirations to swim the channel before she'd died, so there had been no questioning the fact that they all had to be swimmers, too.

'One, two, three, four, five, six...'

They were all focusing on the counting when they heard a purring noise in the water.

'What the heck is *that*?' Sam shrieked.

'Don't worry,' Pip said, 'it sounds like a motor.'

Treading water, they looked around. Deep shades of orange were staining the sky. The shadows in the water were long gone and had been replaced by darkness all around them.

Have we moved at all? wondered Zoe hopelessly.

'Over there!' breathed Pip, lifting his arm and waving. 'Everyone, shout and wave!'

Panic and relief collided as the children all started to wave and shout, '*Tolong, Pak! Tolong*!' (Help, Sir! Help!)

In that moment, the silhouette of the prahu in the distance was the most beautiful thing Zoe had ever seen. They kept shouting.

'Has he seen us?' Mandy panted.

'Look, he's turned his head! He's looking at us!' Sam rejoiced.

The kids waved and shouted crazily. The nose of the prahu shifted and pointed in their direction. 'He can see us! He can see us!' Diana gasped.

Dropping their hands, treading water, and waiting as they drifted in the silent, dark water, they watched as the prahu inched closer, the noise of the motor growing louder as it neared.

'*Apa saja yang kalian lagi lakukan disini?*' (What on earth are you doing here?) said the fisherman, looking incredulous as he cut the motor and drifted towards them.

'*Kami lagi berusaha berenang ke Papa Theo dari Pulau Putri,*' answered Pip. (We're swimming from Pulau Putri to Papa Theo.) '*Tetapi, kami 'jadi cape. Tolong bantu?*' (But we're tired. Can you please help us?)

Tutting and shaking his head, the fisherman began to lecture them. '*Untung kalian tidak tenggelam. Pegang pada cadiknya.*' (Lucky you didn't drown! Hang onto the outriggers.)

Too happy to feel chastened, the children clung onto the outriggers with relief. Tightening their grip as the fisherman started the motor,

they felt the drag as the prahu moved forward, towing them towards the island, a shower, and supper.

Slowing as he approached the rim of the reef, the fisherman said '*Yah. Sudah. Berenang dari sini.*' (Okay, enough. You can swim from here.)

Waving and shouting, '*Terima kasih bapak. Selamat malam!*' (Thank you. Have a nice evening!) the children let go of the outriggers. They swam over the reef and into the lagoon with renewed energy. They couldn't wait to get out of the water.

'My arms are completely dead,' sighed Diana.

'My fingers are like prunes,' said Zoe.

'I am never doing what you say ever again, Pip,' Sam huffed, lying back on the sand.

'At least you know you'll always have an adventure with me!' Pip answered with a smirk on his face.

Rolling their eyes and laughing, the children dragged their heavy limbs back to their cottages, eager to rinse the salt and sand from their bodies and get dry.

'I can't believe we did that,' Mandy said as the girls walked towards the restaurant.

Relishing being dry and the feel of the soft fabric of her sarong, Zoe said, 'It was a pretty dumb thing to do. We're so lucky that prahu came by.'

Overhearing and catching up, Pip said, 'We would have made it. It might have been dark, but we would have made it.'

'You don't know that,' Diana frowned.

'Doesn't matter now, though, does it? We're okay,' Zoe interrupted, sensing the beginnings of an argument.

They walked the rest of the way in silence.

Margie and Charles were already there, waiting.

'There you are!' Margie smiled. 'I was wondering where you were. What did you get up to today?'

Dragging their chairs out and settling at the

table, the children looked at each other guiltily, silently wondering who was going to tell the story.

'Well?' Charles pushed.

'Well...' Diana murmured. 'We swam to Pulau Putri and back.'

Spluttering, Margie exclaimed, 'You did *what*?'

Feeling a bit foolish, the children sank back in their chairs.

After a few moments of silence, Charles said, 'It looks like you know it was a silly and dangerous thing to do.'

'Especially without telling us you were doing it!' added Margie.

The children nodded solemnly. It *did* seem like a silly thing to have done. Zoe had tears in her eyes. She felt exhausted and hungry.

Charles scanned the children. 'I bet you're starving,' he sighed.

'I could eat a horse,' said Sam, grinning.

'Well, let's order then!'

Later, full, exhausted, and relieved, Zoe

sank back against her pillows and gazed at the blue-lit fish tank. Her eyelids grew heavy, and within moments of their heads hitting their pillows, every child in every bed in Cottages One and Three fell into a deep slumber.

Chapter Three

'We only have two more days before we head back to Jakarta,' Zoe said despondently. She loved the rhythm of the days at the islands.

Diana and Mandy were both absorbed in their books. Zoe wasn't sure if they'd heard her.

It was another beautiful day, and the water looked inviting, but after yesterday's adventure, no one really felt like swimming.

Deciding to look for the boys, Zoe left Diana and Mandy reading in the shade on their bamboo sun loungers. 'Have you seen the boys?' Zoe asked Margie and Charles when she found them sitting on the porch of their cottage, playing a game of gin rummy.

'They mentioned something about looking for dragons,' replied Margie, not taking her eyes off her cards.

'Okay. Thanks.' *I bet they're at the rubbish tip,* Zoe thought as she headed in its direction, hidden in the middle of the island.

As she wandered along the sandy tracks, the trees and plants grew wilder and denser. Zoe always started to feel a little nervous whenever she was exploring on her own. Some of the Komodo dragons were huge. If they bit you, the danger wasn't losing a toe; it was the infection that came with it.

The world seemed quieter in a heavy sort of way under the forest canopy. The whisperings of the wind and the lapping of the sea faded with each step into the forest.

Suddenly, there was the faint crack of a twig snapping. Zoe stopped. Her heartbeat quickened. The coins of sunlight that had found their way through the forest canopy felt hot on her bare shoulders. She held her breath and listened with her whole body. She was alert, primed and ready to run back to the safety of the beach and cottages, when she heard quiet voices. Breathing a sigh of relief, she identified the noise as the boys coming back along the track. She waited for them and said, 'Hello,' as they appeared. They were all tanned and, as usual, wearing nothing but their swimming shorts. Sam's blonde hair looked almost white in the sun. 'What've you got there?'

Pip was casually holding a small Komodo dragon to his chest like it was the most natural thing in the world. The claws of its right foot were clinging to his shoulder and the other to the side of his chest. Its long tail curled around his leg. 'A baby monitor lizard,' Pip replied nonchalantly.

'It doesn't *look* like much of a baby,' Zoe remarked as she inspected it. Its body was as long as Pip's torso. 'Isn't it a Komodo dragon?'

'Komodos only live on Flores Island. This is an Asian water monitor. They can grow up to around two meters in length, and are the second heaviest after the Komodo dragon. So that's probably why people get them confused.'

Watching its blue split tongue dart out, Zoe asked, 'What if it bites you?'

'It'll hurt,' said Pip with a grin. Sam and Ben laughed out loud. Zoe noticed there was a nervous edge to it. 'Actually, interesting fact: it's thought that the juvenile lizards are slightly venomous, so I'd rather not get bitten. But this one seems calm enough.'

'What are you going to do with it?' asked Zoe, not surprised that they were having this conversation at all.

'Show Mum and Dad and then let it go,' Pip shrugged.

The children walked in single file along the narrow track with Pip leading the way, still holding the lizard. Zoe watched it dart its tongue out again over Pip's shoulder, feeling a little unnerved.

When they arrived, Charles leaned back in his chair and laughed. 'Trust you to come back with a big lizard, Pip!'

Margie shrieked and jumped. 'Good lord, Pip! How did you catch that?'

'By its tail,' Pip said simply.

Still laughing, Charles said, 'Well, bring it here. Let's have a closer look.'

After everyone had inspected the lizard and admired its yellow spots, Pip put it down on the sand.

'So long as it doesn't go into the cottage…' muttered Margie, eyeing it warily. They all watched as the monitor lizard paused, as though to assess the situation, before scurrying away.

The next morning was glorious. Zoe thought that it seemed such a shame to be leaving while the water was glittering like it was.

She was sitting precariously on their bags, which were piled up at the end of the pier, watching the preparations. The boat they were taking back to Ancol Marina was much smaller than the double-hulled catamaran they had come out on. Charles had chartered it just for them.

'Ah-ha! How sporting! A Rodman Walkaround. Three hundred horsepower!' Charles said suddenly, stopping beside Zoe to admire the boat moored portside. Charles had always loved boats, and worked in shipping. He could identify almost any boat in any marina.

The sun was starting to get hot as the children waited patiently to board. The boys were admiring the school of blue fusiliers swimming between the pylons while Diana and Mandy sunned themselves. *They couldn't be any more tanned than they already are*, Zoe thought, amused.

Zoe watched the captain run the bilge pump and dump water into the sea. She noticed a glossy slick of petrol on the surface of the water. 'Mum, why do they have to spill petrol in the water? It must be terrible for the fish.'

'Oh, it's such a small amount. I'm sure it will dissipate,' Margie replied.

Zoe couldn't help but feel dissatisfied with this answer. She imagined all the boats in all the world spilling just a little bit of petrol every time they filled their engines, and pictured the vast oceans becoming as polluted as the coastal waters around Ancol Marina. She felt the tragedy and travesty of that future keenly.

'Okay. *Siap!*' announced the captain. (Ready!)

All the luggage and their fishing rods had been stored in the small cabin in the hull of the boat. One by one, the group of eight climbed aboard; with the captain, they made a group of nine. With a capacity of ten, the boat was just about at its limit.

Jostling each other to find a prime spot, the boys won the privilege of sitting at the bow of the boat. They couldn't all be at the front, as the boat needed to be balanced in the water. The girls meanwhile sat with Margie on the bench seats at the back and Charles stood beside the captain, looking through the windscreen, feet planted wide apart for balance, looking happy and windswept.

'The captain is missing three fingers,' Zoe

whispered suddenly to her mum, a little alarmed.

'Mm,' Margie said distractedly.

'The captain. His fingers,' Zoe repeated with urgency, nodding her head in his direction.

'Oh, yes! I see.'

'I wonder how he lost them.'

Overhearing their conversation, Charles asked the captain what had happened. Translating for everyone's benefit, Charles said, 'The motor seized one day as a piece of plastic got caught up in the blades. He reached down to pull the plastic free but hadn't turned the motor off. As soon as he loosened the plastic, the blades suddenly spun again and cut all three fingers off in a split second.'

Seeing the horrified looks on the girls' faces, the captain roared with laughter. 'Let it be a lesson,' said Charles. 'Always turn the motor off, whether it's a boat or a lawnmower. Your fingers will always be worse off if you don't.'

Leaning back and absorbing that advice, everyone settled into a peaceful silence as the boat motored smoothly over the reef and out into the deep blue. The islands drifted by as they made their way out into the Java Sea to cross the deep shipping channel to make their way home.

And then, it happened almost without warning.

The crash of the boat into the trough of the swell shook everyone's bones.

The boys had moved to the back of the boat and sat huddled together in one corner. The girls were huddled together in the other. Zoe was sitting at Margie's feet, and she unconsciously curled her arm around Margie's leg.

Zoe sensed the tension in Margie and braced as the boat powered up the face of the swell and then crashed into the next trough, and the one after that.

Charles, still standing by the captain at the steering wheel, was holding fast to the handles. His feet were wide apart, his whole body braced and ready. Zoe watched his legs straighten as the boat powered up the face of the swell and bend to absorb the crash. He turned his head briefly to check on everyone, his expression grim. He exchanged a look with Margie which Zoe couldn't read but understood the meaning of, and started to feel frightened.

Noticing a tugging sensation, she turned to see Margie tying the straps of her life jacket to the straps on Diana's life jacket. Mandy's had already been tied to Diana's other strap. Margie then wound her fingers around the shoulder strap of Diana's life jacket and gripped so hard that her knuckles turned white almost instantly.

Zoe looked over at the boys and noticed that they had tied themselves together as well. Even Pip's face was pale and peaked.

Looking back to the front of the boat, it didn't seem possible for the swell to get any bigger. But it did. The wall of water in front of them towered into the sky. The captain leaned forward, as if willing the boat to climb to the peak, gripping the steering wheel.

The motor roared and whined.

They made it. This time.

The captain pulled the engine back. As the boat paused at the peak of the swell, it sounded like the engine had suddenly cut out; all was quieter than before. Zoe looked around and could see the enormous hills of water stretching out in every direction, rolling into the horizon.

It felt like the boat teetered for a moment before plunging down the face of the swell and crashing into the trough. Zoe felt her teeth clack together and her knee bang and scrape on the floor of the boat. All she could see was walls of water around them, steel grey, shadowy, and menacing. Salt spray whipped them all.

Margie's expression was bleak, her face pale. She continued to grip Diana's life jacket with one hand and the grab rail with the other. She checked that the children's life jackets were still firmly tied together every few minutes.

The boys had by now shuffled closer. Zoe felt Pip slip his fingers through the shoulder strap of her life jacket and grip hard. She imagined his knuckles were as white as Margie's.

All they could do was hold onto each other, brace for each crash, and hold their breath as they willed the boat to make it to the peak of each swell.

Zoe recalled the stories Charles had told them about the Java Sea; how it had been a trading route for centuries. The Java Sea was connected to both the Indian Ocean and the South China Sea, which meant the marine traffic was always high. It also meant that the seafloor was littered with shipwrecks. The Allied forces lost five ships in a battle with the Japanese there in World War II. It was one of the costliest battles of that war. Charles had said that the wrecks became valuable habitats for corals and marine life and that scuba divers loved to explore them. He had dived a few of the wrecks himself. As she remembered these stories, Zoe couldn't help but imagine their boat, which felt so small in this vast body of water, joining the detritus and broken hulls of ships which haunted the seafloor. Hot tears pricked her eyes.

The engine whined as they climbed another

wall of water. This time, when the boat crashed into the trough, the casing of the internal wall fell off and clattered to the floor.

No one could do anything about it.

It slid around as the boat lurched and rolled, and with each crash, more items fell as screws came loose. The boat was literally falling apart.

Zoe looked up to see Margie was crying. Everyone was salt-caked and drenched from sea spray. Margie's tears joined at her chin and dripped freely. She continued to grip onto Diana's life jacket and the handrail, flexing and bracing with every climb and crash down the swell, her gaze steady but unfocused.

It seemed to go on forever, but the boat somehow kept going. The engine kept powering them up each swell and stayed afloat after each crash into the troughs.

Suddenly, almost imperceptibly, the swell grew smaller. Charles glanced around at everyone. His eyes were red from salt spray, but there was a glimmer of hope in them.

Almost as quickly as the swell had risen, the

sea began to flatten. The raging waves retreated; weakened. Margie loosened her grip on Diana's life jacket but still didn't let go. The tension that everyone had been holding in their bodies began to visibly dissipate. The captain's shoulders loosened. Ancol Marina was in sight!

Zoe had never been more relieved to see the brown polluted water and the rickety piers of the marina. As the boat limped towards the shore, Margie finally started undoing the straps of the life jackets with trembling hands. Charles came to help, taking a moment to brush his hand tenderly across Margie's cheek. She closed her eyes and tilted her head into his palm, sighing deeply and shakily with relief. There were no words that could be said in that moment.

Finally, they docked. The captain looked exhausted, his eyes blood-red from the sting of salt spray. Charles put one hand on the captain's shoulder and shook the other with gratitude. '*Terima kasih,*' he said emotionally. (Thank you.)

One by one, the children gravely thanked

the captain, disembarked, and made their way to the car with quaking legs. Exhaustion and relief flooded them all. Margie kept hugging and touching the children as though she couldn't believe they were all alright.

Later, when everyone was at home and showered and dry, barely a word was spoken as everyone shovelled hot spoonful after hot spoonful of shepherd's pie into their mouths. Margie and Charles held hands throughout the meal, casting their eyes over the children in between mouthfuls. Finally, Charles spoke. 'You were all very brave today. Well done.'

'That was so scary,' Diana murmured.

'Yes, it was. It's a good reminder of how dangerous the sea can be, though, isn't it?' Charles nodded. 'But the main thing is that we made it. We're all safe, and now we have another adventure story to tell our friends!' He cracked a grin.

Margie closed her eyes, shook her head, smiled weakly, and said:

'Another adventure indeed!'

SUKEY THE GOOSE

Chapter One

'Oh my goodness! She's so fluffy!' Zoe exclaimed.

'Happy birthday!' Samantha cheered, who at that moment was Zoe's favourite friend in the whole world.

They were bending over a small carboard box which moments before had been bound closed with twine. The bottom was lined with newspaper, and sitting in the corner was the most beautiful yellow-and-grey gosling Zoe had ever seen.

Zoe reached in with both hands, gently picked up the chirping bird, and brought it to her face so she could gently rub it against her cheek. 'So soft! Feel it,' Zoe cooed, holding the gosling out to Samantha.

'Yes, she's lovely. I picked out the cutest one for you.' Samantha smiled, stroking the gosling's back.

'Thank you. I love her. She's the best present ever!'

'Let's put her away for now,' said Margie, picking up the box and holding it out for Zoe. 'I'll make sure she has some food and water, and you can check on her after the party.'

Pip and Zoe were celebrating their ninth birthday, and so far, it was shaping up to be wonderful. Throughout the day, in between the games and the cake, Zoe couldn't help but sneak into the garage to peek at the tiny gosling. She did this numerous times, a new friend in tow with every visit.

'Don't handle her too much, darling. She'll get stressed. She needs time to settle in,' Margie reminded Zoe.

'I know. I just can't help it. She's so

adorable!' Zoe squealed, scrunching up her face.

'What colour will she be when she grows up?' asked Zoe's friend, Claire. She and Samantha had been brought along for another peek at the gosling.

'She'll be brown, grey, and white,' Samantha said knowingly, who had a whole gaggle of geese at home. While their gander was white with blue eyes, most of the geese were brown and grey with white throats, a black bill, and orange legs and feet.

'You could call her Sukey,' Nancy piped up from a few feet away.

Zoe cocked her head for a moment. 'That's a great suggestion, Nancy. I like that one. Thanks!'

Later, when the party was over, Pip and Zoe showed each other their presents, exclaiming over each and every one. Pip, a little jealous, said, 'I wish *I* got a pet.'

'You got a terrapin last year, remember?' Zoe said.

Acknowledging this with a shrug, Pip

asked, 'What are you going to name your goose?'

'Firstly, she's still a gosling,' Zoe said haughtily, 'but I'm going to call her Sukey. Nancy suggested it. It's perfect, isn't it!'

'S'pose,' he said, reaching for the last of his gifts.

The next morning, Zoe was discussing where Sukey could live with her mum.

'Well, we have an enclosure which isn't being used. That could be where she sleeps at night, but she can roam the garden during the day,' suggested Margie.

'Really? That sounds perfect. Thanks, Mum!' Zoe said, hugging her.

'She'll need to stay in the crate in the garage to begin with, though. Once she gets her feathers, she can go into the enclosure.'

Each night, Zoe put a towel on top of the newspaper for Sukey to snuggle into, as well as another over the top of one half of the crate so that Sukey would feel safe and warm during the night. That morning, after Zoe's conversation with Margie, Zoe lifted the towel off the crate to find Sukey tucked into the corner, her beak nestled in her downy feathers. 'You've made a royal mess in there,' Zoe said, inspecting the upended water tray, soaked newspaper, scattered food, and poop. 'And you poop a lot for a little creature!'

Lifting her out and holding her at arms-length, Zoe took the chirping gosling out to the garden, where she had filled a big, round bucket with water. Laughing at Sukey's feet paddling the air, Zoe gently placed her in the water. Ducking and chirping, Sukey's swam around happily in the sunshine, washing off the night's dirt, while Zoe sat cross-legged on the grass by the bucket and stroked Sukey each time she paddled by.

After a while, Zoe put Sukey on the grass so she could do some grazing. It wasn't long before Sukey sat down and closed her eyes, enjoying the sunshine.

'Time for a snooze, eh, Sukey?'

Zoe made a sling to carry Sukey in by tying an old sarong around her body like a sash (over her right shoulder and under her left arm). Once she'd tucked Sukey's bottom under her arm, she realized, with delight, that Sukey could look over the edge of the sling and chirp happily away.

Zoe could still remember the snug feeling of being carried like this on Ibu Marsi's hip. Ibu Marsi had been the children's nanny since they were born. The sarong had been tight around her back and had effortlessly supported her weight, just like how many Indonesian babies were carried every day.

Zoe sat down at the table for lunch with Sukey happily snuggled in her sling. She started feeding Sukey pieces of bread soaked in milk, and was gleefully watching her gulp it down when she was suddenly startled by her mother's exclamation: 'Go and put that goose away! You can't eat your lunch with her on your lap! For heaven's sake, it's unhygienic! Put her away and wash your hands.'

'But Mum, I'll eat with my right hand! She's all snug and happy and getting used to me!' Zoe argued.

'No discussion, Zoe. Do it now!'

Huffing with disappointment, Zoe reluctantly left the table to put Sukey in her crate.

Once everyone was settled back at the table, Margie said, 'Right, we need to lay down some rules. No animals at the table, okay? We need to have some decorum around here. I thought that was clear after you sat down to supper with that bat hanging from your finger earlier this year, Zoe.'

Pip and Zoe grinned. Their neighbour, Joyo, had climbed the palm tree and caught a baby microbat for Zoe to play with. The children had loved it. Its fur was so soft, its wings were covered with a fine velvety down, and its face was adorable: tiny and inquiring, made comical by its enormous ears twitching this way and that.

'It was cool how it climbed up your T-shirt

with the little hooks at the elbow bends in its wings,' Pip giggled.

'Yes, and how it hung upside down from my finger! My arm got so tired. That's why I rested my elbow on the table, Mum: so that the bat could hang and my arm could rest.'

'Yes, well, I'm glad Joyo put it back in the palm tree with its family,' Margie sighed.

'What about that atlas moth, Pip? Do you remember that one?' Zoe asked excitedly.

'That was super-cool,' Pip grinned, eyes brightening. Sensing Margie's disapproving gaze, he added, 'Mum, we found the chrysalis in the garden and only had it for a few days. Zoe brought it with her to the table when we were having supper...' He paused, expecting to be scolded. Margie rolled her eyes, but there was a smile there. 'Anyway,' he went on, 'the chrysalis started to wriggle on the table, so we stopped eating and watched it. After a while, this brown liquid came out of it...' Pip paused and looked at his mum again. Pip and Zoe giggled at the disgusted look on her face. She shook her head, but Pip, undeterred, pressed on. 'So, anyway, this brown liquid came out of the chrysalis, and slowly, the moth broke the chrysalis shell and wriggled out. Its wings were all crumpled up and damp, so Zoe put her hand under its feet and let it crawl onto her hand before letting it crawl onto her chest.'

'Yes, it was amazing, Mum,' Zoe nodded. 'It stayed there gently unfurling and slowly flapping its wings to dry them. And then after a while, its wings were fully open. Its wings were so big that they spread across my chest and

almost reached my shoulders! It seemed to take *ages.'*

'And then what did you do with it?' Margie asked, arching an eyebrow.

'Well, I carefully got up and we went outside, and we released it in the garden,' Zoe said.

'Apparently, atlas moths only live for a couple of days,' Pip chipped in.

'That's sad,' said Zoe reflectively. 'I didn't know that.'

No one said anything for a moment. Then, Margie said, 'Thank you sharing that story with me, but back to what I was saying before: from now on, no more animals at the table, please.'

'Okay, Mum,' Pip and Zoe chimed together, knowing full well that it was a promise they would find very hard to keep.

Sukey grew quickly over the next few weeks. At first, she looked ragged as her lovely soft down started turning into feathers, but before long, she grew into an elegant goose. Her long neck arched gracefully, the snow-white feathers down the front of her neck were smooth and soft to stroke, and above her black bill was a soft bump (a 'basal knob', according to Pip) that was soft and warm to touch, yielding slightly when Zoe stroked it. The brown stripe down the back of her head and neck gave way to precise and pretty brown-and-grey markings on her back and wing feathers, and under her wings and around her stomach the feathers were soft, thick, and downy.

'You could make a wonderful goose down pillow out of those feathers,' Zoe's father, Charles, often joked, much to Zoe's consternation.

Sukey swam in the pool with the children frequently, and when things were calm, she would happily sit on Zoe's lap nibbling at the earrings in her ears and playfully biting at her fingers, leaving small scratches from the sharp, serrated edges of her bill (which were perfect for cutting the grass she grazed on all day!).

Sukey was mostly left to wander around the

garden, grazing, and she kindly left wet blobs of poop everywhere. Margie cursed whenever she stepped in them.

One afternoon, after the children had returned from school, Zoe went to look for Sukey. *'Ibu marsi, dimana Sukey?'* (Where is Sukey?) she asked. She hadn't been able to find her anywhere.

'Lihat di sebelah kolam ikan. Ia telah membuat sarang baru di sana,' (Look by the fishpond. She has made a new nest there) Ibu Marsi replied.

Zoe went back to the pond and looked behind the philodendrons. 'There you are, Sukey!'

Sukey was sitting contentedly on a large nest. Zoe crawled over to her and sat beside her. She stroked her back as Sukey honked gently, curling her head around to nibble on Zoe's leg.

They sat companionably for a while, until Sukey got up to have a drink at the pond.

'Oh, an egg!' Zoe exclaimed excitedly. 'It's *enormous!'*

Sukey had laid a perfectly white egg that

was at least four times the size of a chicken egg. Leaving Sukey, Zoe crawled out from behind the philodendrons and went inside to find her mum. She needed to share the news!

'Mum, Sukey has laid the most enormous egg! What should we do?' she announced breathlessly when she found her.

'Oh! How lovely. Well, it'll just go off if you leave it there, as it can't possibly be fertilised without a gander. They're quite a delicacy, so we should eat it,' Margie replied.

'Oh, of course. I didn't think of that!'

When Zoe went back to take the egg, Sukey was back on her nest. 'I'm just going to take that egg. Okay, Sukey?' Zoe said soothingly as she tried to reach under the bird to claim it.

Sukey honked aggressively and bit at Zoe's hand.

'Oh. You don't think it's going to hatch, do you?' Zoe sighed, trying to reach for it again.

But apparently, she did. Sukey wouldn't have any of it and hissed at Zoe, guarding her egg with ruffled feathers and an angry honk.

'Okay, then. I'll try later. I'll leave you to sit on it, you silly goose.'

Once she was sat down at the table for an afternoon tea of fried bananas, Zoe sighed, 'Sukey won't let me take it.' She took a bite of the fried banana and exhaled with contentment. It was one of her favourite snacks: fresh ripe bananas sliced and dipped into a vanilla flavoured batter, fried, and served with a dusting of icing sugar. With sugar powdered around her mouth, Zoe added, 'I'll take it when she gets up for something to eat or drink.' She thought for a moment and then added, 'Considering she's being so protective of her egg, do you think she thinks it will hatch?'

'Yes, probably,' Margie answered. 'I'm sure she's lonely. They're not solitary animals.'

Pip had joined them at the table by this point. 'What's happening?' he asked.

'Sukey has laid an egg. It can't possibly be fertilised, so Mum suggested we eat it like a chicken egg. I tried to take it but she's guarding it quite possessively. She hissed at me and tried to bite me.'

'Oh. I'll come with you after we've finished eating to see if I can help.'

After they'd taken their dishes to the kitchen and thanked Marsi for their afternoon tea, they went to find Sukey. 'She's built her nest behind the fishpond, against the house,' Zoe explained. 'It's a lovely spot for a nest, really. Under the shade of the tree and behind the philodendrons.'

Pip and Zoe crawled behind the philodendrons and found Sukey still sat on her nest. She honked at them and adjusted herself irritably, fluffing her feathers.

'Mum said that maybe she's lonely. I think she needs a mate. I wonder if we could borrow Samantha's gander for a while?' Zoe pondered.

'That's a good idea,' Pip murmured, stroking Sukey.

'I'll just pick her up and you snatch the egg, okay?'

Pip nodded.

Zoe crouched over Sukey, making her honk

in alarm. Undeterred, Zoe courageously reached her arms under Sukey's breast, picked her up, and held her to her chest, pressing Sukey's wings in with her elbows. Sukey paddled her feet in the air and honked angrily. 'Grab the egg, Pip! She's so strong,' Zoe grunted as Sukey struggled against her, trying to flap her wings and bite Zoe's hands.

'Got it!' Pip announced. 'It's *huge!*'

'Be careful with it!' Zoe said as she put Sukey down awkwardly. Sukey flapped her wings and honked in indignation. 'Sorry, Sukey.'

'The mozzies are biting,' Pip said as he slapped at his leg with one hand, balancing the goose egg in the other.

'Okay, let's go in,' Zoe said, slapping at her own itching neck.

'Gosh, that *is* huge!' Margie exclaimed as she stared at the large white goose egg presented to her by the children.

'I think I should invite Samantha over to eat

it with us,' Zoe said.

'Good idea. Let's keep it in the fridge until the weekend.'

Chapter Two

On Saturday morning, after Samantha had slept over, the girls gathered in the kitchen to ceremoniously prepare the goose egg for breakfast.

'How shall we cook it?' Zoe mused.

'Well, we can make an omelette, or scramble it, or we can boil it or fry it,' Margie said.

At that moment, Pip rushed into the kitchen with his hands cupped in front of him. 'I found some pigeon eggs!' he exclaimed. 'We should cook these, too, and compare the sizes!'

Zoe and Samantha looked at the two tiny eggs in Pip's hands. 'Where did you find them?'

Zoe asked.

'I just had a look in the nests in the pigeon loft, and they were there! We have so many pigeons now that it won't matter if we eat these eggs. They weren't there yesterday—I checked—so they're definitely fresh.'

Even more excited now, the children agreed that frying the eggs would be the best way to compare the sizes. So, Margie got out two frying pans and, after adding the oil and butter, cracked the goose egg into one.

'Ooh, look! It's filling the pan up completely!' Samantha said as they watched the white of the goose egg spread to the edge of the pan.

'Look at that yolk!' added Zoe. 'It's enormous!'

Indeed, the dark gold dome of the yolk was almost the size of an orange.

Margie and Pip prepared the second frying pan and cracked the pigeon eggs in. Their diminutive size was equally impressive to the children.

'They're so perfect and tiny. They could be for fairies,' Zoe smiled.

For good measure, they cooked a chicken egg, too. Because why not?

The children sat at the table and *ooh*ed and *ahh*ed as the eggs were served. A hot pile of buttered toast was stacked in a basket between them.

'Sam and I will halve one of the pigeon eggs, and you can have the other one, seeing as you found them. And then we'll share the goose egg equally. Sound fair?' Zoe said.

Pip and Samantha agreed. And so the children divided up the eggs, laughing at the mess the yolk of the goose egg made.

'Okay, let's see how different the pigeon and goose egg tastes to the chicken egg,' Pip grinned.

It turned out that the eggs tasted pretty much exactly the same to the children, especially with a bit of tomato sauce on the side.

'How are they?' asked Margie, coming to the table with her coffee.

'Delicious,' the children said through full mouths.

'Would you like to try some?' Samantha asked.

'Thank you, but no. You look like you're enjoying them,' she smiled.

None of the children could finish their share of the goose egg.

'So. Full,' groaned Pip as he leant back in his chair.

'Me too,' the girls said simultaneously.

Later, as they wandered around the garden to digest their breakfast, they spotted Sukey grazing on the grass. 'Let's check her nest!' Zoe suggested.

They stooped behind the philodendrons to see if Sukey had laid any more eggs, but discovered, to their surprise, that she had rolled one of the white painted stones that decorated the edge of the pond into her nest.

'Oh, no!' Zoe cried. 'Poor Sukey! She thinks she still has her egg.'

From then on, Sukey never laid another egg. She just continued to sit on the white painted stones. Every time Zoe removed the stones from the nest, Sukey rolled them back in with her beak.

'Mum, what should we do?' Zoe asked one day, concerned. 'Sukey is convinced she's sitting on eggs, and won't leave her nest.'

'I'm not sure. I'll have a think about it,' Margie frowned.

Zoe felt guilty for taking Sukey's egg in the first place, even though she knew it would just have gone off.

A few days later, when Zoe arrived home from school, Margie called her into the kitchen to show her two new goose eggs in a little basket.

'Where did you get them?' Zoe gasped. 'Did Sukey lay more eggs?'

'No. We managed to get fertile goose eggs from the markets. Go and pop them under Sukey, and let's see what happens.'

Carefully, Zoe took the eggs, found Sukey sitting on her stones, and crouched next to her. 'Hello, Sukey,' Zoe said gently, reaching out and stroking her. She had brought some grain and a little bowl of water. Sukey happily pecked the grain in Zoe's palm and drank from the bowl without leaving her nest. Distracted by the food and accustomed to Zoe's visits, Sukey's only reaction to Zoe pushing her hand under her downy feathers and nestling the eggs between Sukey's legs was a slight adjustment of her body.

'How did you go?' Margie asked upon

Zoe's return.

'Well, she barely noticed me putting the eggs underneath her. I didn't take the stones. I'll take them next time she's off her nest.'

'You understand there's no guarantee that the eggs will hatch, right?' Margie said, looking Zoe pointedly in the eye.

'Yes, I understand. I hope they will, though. She is so dedicated to nesting. She must really want a baby!'

A few weeks later, it was obvious the eggs were rotten.

'What a pity,' Margie sighed.

'She's rolled another stone onto the nest,' Zoe said incredulously. 'The poor thing!'

'Well, the next step in the plan is to borrow Samantha's gander,' Margie shrugged. 'If they'll agree to lending him to us, of course.'

Zoe brightened with excitement at the prospect of goslings, and was thrilled when it was agreed that the gander could come and stay for a while. The blue-eyed white gander arrived the very next weekend.

It was a disaster.

Sukey honked and hissed and fussed at his presence. Whenever he came close to her, she hissed and bit him in rage.

Margie and Zoe stood watching them one afternoon with frowns on their faces.

'What a fuss! I'm not sure I can stand the noise for much longer,' Margie said, shaking her head. 'Sukey does not like him at all! The poor gander. He looks a bit defeated.'

The gander, handsome as he was, followed Sukey around the garden, to no avail, honking forlornly.

Two weeks later, he was back in a box heading back to Samantha's house to re-join his gaggle.

One day, when Pip and Zoe arrived home from school, they heard wild honking and noise coming from Sukey's enclosure as soon as they opened the car doors. Looking alarmed, Zoe said, 'I wonder what's happening!'

Dropping their school bags in the garage, Pip and Zoe ran back along the driveway and past the pond, cassia tree, and porch. They sprinted to the enclosure in the shade of the mango tree, and couldn't believe what they saw.

'Oh my goodness!' Zoe exclaimed.

Locked in the enclosure was Sukey, fussing and honking and running away from two little goslings, who were desperately trying to seek shelter under her wings. The poor little things tripped and fell over their feet in their clumsy efforts to sit under Sukey, undeterred by her pecking and hissing.

'Why is she making such a fuss?' Zoe asked Margie, who had joined them to watch the commotion.

'It's a big adjustment for her,' Margie shrugged. 'I guess she doesn't understand where they came from. She's been sitting on those stones for so long that I thought we should get her some babies. I hoped that she would adopt them.' She paused, observing the chaos. 'And I think she will. She just needs a little time.

We'll keep them in the enclosure together for a few days and see what happens. We've set up the crate on its side and put some shredded paper and straw in there so that the babies can snuggle up together if Sukey won't let them nest with her.'

Over supper that night, they could still hear the geese honking and fussing. The pauses between Sukey's loud honks were filled with the desperate chirps of the goslings. Feeling sad, Zoe said, 'Poor little goslings. I really hope Sukey adopts them.'

A few days later, she got her wish. Seemingly overnight, Sukey had transformed into a protective mother goose! As the babies waddled around the garden, Sukey practically walked sideways, bending her neck around the goslings so she could protect them from every potential danger. The goslings huddled around her feet and disappeared beneath her at every opportunity.

'I guess we can name them now,' Pip grinned while they watched Sukey and the goslings waddle around like a single organism. 'I think she definitely considers them her babies.'

'Yup. Thank goodness,' Zoe breathed. 'Maybe we should call them Huey and Duey in memory of Louie.'

The twins had a habit of naming their pets after Disney characters. The characters from *The Jungle Book* were the most popular. Their rottweiler had been named Bagheera, Zoe's cat had been named after Sher Khan, and Pip was often nicknamed Mowgli for being such a jungle boy.

Louie was a runner duck who'd mysteriously fallen off the roof into the pool one day and unwittingly become part of the family. But that's a story for another day.

It wasn't long before the goslings turned into lovely white geese. The trio were inseparable. They would fossick in the grass, swim in the swimming pool, and honk loudly whenever they were disturbed.

Not all was sunshine and rainbows, though:

Margie still took to cursing every time they left deposits on the porch or the back veranda. She couldn't help but cry out with disgust when she saw the coping of the swimming pool splattered with goose poop. 'Those geese are so noisy and make such a mess!' she grumbled. 'They ate all my seedlings today. I'm getting sick of them, you know.'

'Sorry, Mum,' Zoe murmured with a grimace.

She knew Margie was irritated, but she didn't for a moment think that anything would change. They were her pets, after all.

Over the next year, Pip and Zoe enjoyed swimming with the geese and followed them around the garden. They were the centre of attention whenever friends came over to play.

One day, observing the melee unfold in the pool full of children and geese, Margie muttered to Charles, 'This is getting out of control. Someone is going to get sick, swimming with the geese pooping in the water. There's only so

much chlorine we can add…' Her voice trailed away.

'Yes. Probably time to set some boundaries,' Charles nodded.

Just as Charles went to declare the new rule—no more geese in the pool—Zoe had hauled herself out of the pool to get away from the nominated 'Marco' in their wild game of Marco Polo. In her haste to get away, she slipped on a fresh dollop of goose poop, falling hard onto her back and cracking the back of her head on the edge of the pool.

She sat up woozily, the dull ache in her head instantly making her feel sick. She gingerly touched the back of her head, which was intensely tender and painful. Bringing her fingers in front of her eyes, it took a moment for her vision to focus, and when it finally did, she saw blood coating her skin. She suddenly felt even more faint and woozy.

She was vaguely aware of the commotion going on around her as the children were ordered out of the pool and Margie yelled, 'Pip, get me that towel!' Charles was meanwhile gently scooping her up and holding her head against his chest, and she heard one of her friends (she couldn't tell who) whisper in shock, 'There's so much blood.'

Closing her eyes, she surrendered to the feeling of her dad wrapping her in a towel against him and someone pressing something against the back of her head. She winced and moaned in pain.

The next thing she knew, she was on her dad's lap in the backseat of the car, her mum driving and cursing at the Jakarta traffic. At one point, she dimly heard her dad say, 'Pip, keep the pressure on,' and moaned as she felt increased pressure on the back of her head. It seared with pain.

As they arrived at the hospital, Zoe saw from under her heavy lids that Pip was still in his bathers and barefoot. She still felt incredibly nauseous and dimly noted that tears were falling down her face, yet she didn't feel like she was crying.

Before long, Zoe was lying on her side on a hospital bed. It seemed like dozens of people were moving about, talking and planning. The doctor flashed his torchlight into her eyes, making her blink and recoil a little. 'Good,' he said quietly. She felt the back of her head being sprayed with something cold. 'Topical anaesthesia,' she heard someone say.

She saw Pip standing against the pink curtain, still barefoot and in his bathers, staring at her with wide-eyed concern.

Zoe cried out as the doctors started to clean and prepare her wound for stitching, squeezing her eyes closed. She braced herself. Her mum held her hands and her dad held her foot and rubbed her back gently.

'We'll keep her under observation until we can be confident that her concussion is just that,' Zoe heard a doctor say. She'd been answering all the questions they'd asked correctly, much to everyone's relief.

Kissing her tenderly on the forehead, Charles said, 'See you at home, possum. You were very brave.'

Pip added, 'See you, sis,' hesitating before giving her a peck on the cheek.

With that, Charles and Pip went home, leaving Margie to sit with Zoe, stroking her hand reassuringly. After a while, Margie asked how she was feeling.

'Sore,' Zoe whimpered.

'I'm sure it's *very* sore, my darling,' Margie responded sadly. Unable to wait a moment longer, she added, 'I'm sorry to bring this up now, but we need to talk about your geese.'

Zoe blinked slowly in agreement.

Margie went on, 'It's Dad's and my fault that this happened. We should have seen the danger. We should never have allowed the geese in the pool, not just because of the slipping hazard their poop has become, but also because you'll get sick swimming with them. We need to think about what to do next, okay, sweetheart?'

Zoe tried to nod but it hurt her head too much. Noticing Zoe wince, Margie said, 'We'll focus on you getting better first, okay? We'll talk about the geese another time. Just mull it over, if you can.'

Chapter Three

'*How* many stitches?' Samantha exclaimed in awe.

'Ten,' Zoe replied.

'Wow. I didn't realize it was *that* bad!'

'Mum and Dad have banned the geese from the pool,' Zoe said sadly, 'and they think that maybe we need to rehome them sooner than planned…'

Samantha had come to visit Zoe and had brought a homemade 'get well soon' cake—a delicious chocolate cake with velvety chocolate icing. They were already onto their second slice.

'Maybe we could have them? Although I

did overhear my parents saying something about our gaggle being too big,' Samantha said through a mouthful of cake. There was icing on her chin, and some crumbs dropped to the table from her mouth as she talked.

Once they felt too sick to eat any more, they wandered into the garden to check on the geese. They found them grazing around the frangipani trees. Zoe sat on the grass and leaned against one of the trees, pulling Sukey into her lap. Sukey settled down and honked quietly. Zoe tucked her hand under Sukey's wing to stroke her thick downy feathers. Samantha meanwhile sat and leaned against the trunk of the next closest frangipani, watching Huey and Duey grazing nonchalantly around them.

'Mum also said that seeing as I'll be going to boarding school soon in Australia, we might as well rehome the geese during the next school holidays,' Zoe sighed, bringing Sukey closer.

Samantha would be going to boarding school, too, but in England.

The girls sat in silence, contemplating what

lay ahead.

'The holidays are only weeks away. It feels too soon,' Zoe finally said quietly.

'I know. It feels like everything is going to change forever,' Samantha murmured.

Later that night, just before heading to bed, Zoe said to Margie, 'You know, Mum, I think it would be best for the geese to join a gaggle somewhere. Maybe Samantha's gaggle.' She paused for a moment. 'Or do you remember Eddy up at Puncak, who manages the cottage up there? He had geese in his village. It would be nice for the geese to be in the countryside. There's that beautiful stream by the goose pen we saw that they can swim in. Either way, I'd rather be the one to take them, before I go to boarding school.'

Margie put her arm around Zoe. 'I'm proud of you for always trying to think of what's best for your pets and taking responsibility. I think that would be a good idea. We can visit her whenever we go to Puncak, and I agree: it *would* be much nicer for her to be part of a gaggle and in the countryside.'

Zoe went to bed feeling sad but also calm about the decision that had been made. It was the right thing to do. Plus, it would relieve her parents of the poop and destruction the geese left in their wake!

As she packed the last few things into the boot for their weekend in Puncak, Zoe checked on the geese. They were wrapped in sacks, their heads and necks poking through the hole Joyo had cut in the corner before slipping it over their heads. The sacks were secured with twine to stop the geese from flapping their wings and injuring themselves.

All three were nestled in the footwells at Pip and Zoe's feet. Huey and Duey nipped at each other. Pip and Zoe had grain and water to placate them.

Pip glanced over at Zoe. 'Why are you feeding Sukey again? We haven't even left yet!'

Laughing, Zoe replied, 'I don't know. She looks hungry.'

Once they were settled, and on their way, Zoe stroked Sukey's head tenderly as she watched the Jakarta traffic press around them. It always took longer than expected to get to Puncak. It was impossible to know how the traffic was going to be in Jakarta.

'Puncak' meant 'peak' or 'top'. It was a mountainous pass in West Java, and its hills were striped with row upon row of tea bushes. The tea plantations blanketed the hills as far as the eye could see, and were lined with grassy tracks, which the children could run wildly along. Sometimes they'd hire wiry little mountain ponies whose bridles would be decorated with pom poms and bells and canter, mostly out of control, along the same tracks, bells chiming and knees brushing and snagging against the tea bushes.

Pip and Zoe loved it in Puncak.

One of the first things Zoe would do upon arrival was make a fairy garden. She'd pick ixora, morning glory, and gladiola to create the fairy seats and lanterns that she'd position inside a ring of pebbles. The fairies always left her treats in those gardens, which she would find wet with dew the next morning. Zoe would run from her bed in her nightgown, her feet getting wet and grassy from the early morning dew as she ran past the pool and to the fairy garden in anticipation of what she might find.

Often, at that hour, the clouds would still be low in the valley, retreating slowly over the miles and miles of undulating tea plantations. Zoe would curl up in the mamasan chair and watch the colours in the sky change and shift as the sun rose higher and burned the clouds and mist away, all the while chewing thoughtfully on the sweets she'd found just before the ants did.

It was such a treat to feel almost cold in the mountains after the relentless heat of Jakarta. She loved the fires at night in the hearth; the freezing water in the pool; the crisp, fresh air and the clear running streams with grassy banks, where they would wade and try to catch fish with the kitchen sieve or trap the water striders for close inspection before releasing them back to their elegant waltz on the surface of the water.

After what seemed like hours, they finally drove down the grassy driveway to the cottage they always stayed at. Eddy, the manager, was already there waiting for them. The cottage had been opened up to let the fresh air in, and Zoe noticed the morning glory had grown and draped more luxuriously than ever off the patio roof, reaching almost to the ground in places. The red gladioli were in full bloom in front of the cottage, and the outside air was cool and fresh — a relief after so long in the car.

Sensing a change, the geese began to honk and struggle against their sacks.

'Why don't you two and Eddy take the geese straight to the village? We'll unpack,' Margie suggested to Pip and Zoe.

After being cut free of their sacks, the geese flapped their wings and honked at the indignity they had endured. Once they stopped flapping their wings and drank and ate the water and grain, they started to explore and graze in the garden. After a while, Eddy fetched a long bamboo stick to help guide them down the road. And with that, Pip, Zoe, and Eddy walked slowly in a V shape behind the geese along the road so that they could graze as they went. Zoe watched their tailfeathers comically wag from side to side as they placed each webbed foot carefully in front of the other.

Pip picked at the tea leaves, shredding them between his fingers as they sauntered along. Zoe meanwhile stopped to pick a daisy, which she slid behind her ear.

Eddy kept them all safe on the grassy edge of the road, pressed against the tea bushes while a Kijang loaded with people in its tray ambled by, its motor straining against the hill and the weight it carried.

As they approached the village, Zoe was enthralled by the cottages painted pale blue, green, and pink, like a string of coloured beads against the hillside. The slate roofs were green with moss, and the unevenly stone paved roads

curved charmingly through the village. Grassy tracks disappeared into the plantations at intervals, and they could hear the streams burbling over rocks. The village children gathered around them with curiosity, giggling, pointing, and daring one another to touch Pip's or Zoe's white skin. Pip and Zoe smiled at them and sent them scattering, screeching, and laughing when they spoke in fluent Indonesian.

Once the shock had abated, the crowd gathered around and asked questions, laughing hysterically when Pip and Zoe answered.

By the time they arrived at the muddy enclosure, where a gaggle of geese and a raft of ducks intermingled, honking and quacking loudly, there was a crowd of villagers surrounding them. The geese hesitated, cautious. Then, much to the amusement of the villagers, Zoe squatted down and put her arms around Sukey, drawing her into a hug.

Sukey wrapped her long neck around Zoe's shoulder and stilled.

'Bye, Sukey,' Zoe murmured into her

feathers. 'Thank you for being such a wonderful goose. I love you. I hope you'll be happy here.' Tears threatened to spill down her cheeks. Zoe hugged Huey and Duey in turn and then, straightening, she let Eddy guide the geese into the enclosure, setting off another round of honking and quacking. They watched as the birds circled each other, bowing and dipping their heads in what seemed like an endless communion.

The evening shadows were by now turning the landscape blue. Eddy signalled that it was time to walk home. Turning their backs on Sukey, Huey, and Duey, they bade the villagers goodnight and walked in silence, listening to the night crickets chirping their evening song, a distant owl hooting an early cry, and Eddy's flipflops flipping and flopping softly against the stones.

As they approached the cottage, Zoe looked up and saw that the lights were on inside. Margie had promised them spaghetti bolognaise for supper, their favourite. Full of comfort and love, it never failed to ease the saddest of hearts or enhance the greatest of joys.

Zoe picked a deep red gladiola for her mother as they walked through the shadows on the driveway and towards the open casement windows that were warmly lit from within. It was a perfect vignette of family life, their mother preparing their supper and their dad grating some cheese, two glasses of red wine beside them. The delicious smell reached them before the light spilling out of the kitchen windows did.

Pip elbowed Zoe gently — his way of saying that he was sorry she'd had to say goodbye to her geese. Grateful, she gave him a half smile before heading inside.

BEATING THE TIDE

Chapter One

'Don't touch it! It's super-poisonous,' Zoe warned.

Irritated by his sister's constant cautions, Pip replied, 'I'm not going to touch it. I just want to see it flare its fins.'

Pip and Zoe crouched over the rockpool and watched the lionfish flamboyantly display its quills. Its auburn-and-cream stripes and the dozens of fins fanning around it like streamers in the wind were utterly captivating. Zoe wondered why poisonous animals always seemed to be the most beautiful.

Pip stuck his small net into the rockpool and

waved it about. The fish darted forward, impressively flaring, furling, and unfurling its multitude of fins.

'I can see why it's called a lionfish,' Zoe muttered.

The tide was miles out to sea, exposing the reef and all its treasures. It was a wonderful feeling knowing they had hours of exploring left in the day. The breeze rippled the surface of the water in the rockpools, Zoe's fringe fluttered, and the children, lost in a world of exploration, moved from one rockpool to the next, peering, collecting, and inspecting. Time vanished with the wind.

Pausing to inspect their collection, Zoe exclaimed, 'Oh, you have the lionfish in your bucket!'

'I'll let it go when it's time to go in,' Pip replied defensively.

Zoe was admiring the pretty shells, soft coral, and hermit crabs she had in her bucket when Pip said suddenly, 'Look! Did you see that?'

'Yes! Aren't they pretty? Such a bright electric blue!'

'No, not the fish. There's a moray eel in this pool!' Pip said excitedly, pointing at a clump of muted mauve coral growing on the side of the rockpool just above the sandy bottom.

'Really? Where?'

'It's a small one, but I just saw it go into the hole under that purple coral there.'

Kneeling now, the reef sharp on their knees, they bent lower over the rockpool and watched and waited. The water was crystal clear.

Zoe's face was so close to the water her fringe was getting wet when Pip exclaimed 'There! Can you see it?'

And there, in the shadows of the coral, she could see the moray eel looking up at them. Its skin was a dark muddy green, and its bottom jaw overshot the top, displaying a row of sharp little teeth. Its mouth was slightly open, which gave it a menacing look. Its fin rippled along the length of its body and had a pale blue tinge at the very tip.

It tilted its head to get a better look at them as it inched out from under the coral inquisitively. Keeping its eyes on its intruders, it then curled back in on itself and retreated back into its cave.

'They can bite, you know,' Pip said.

'I bet they can. Look at it! It looks so mean with those sharp teeth,' Zoe gasped. 'A bite from that would *really* hurt. I'm glad it's in the pool and we're safely out here!' She shuddered.

'I don't think they're aggressive, though. Just territorial. But yes, I agree. I wouldn't want to be swimming with it. Hey, watch out for the sea urchins!' he said suddenly as they moved on to the next pool and spotted black sea urchins, their spiky spines sticking stiffly out of their round little bodies. 'Do you remember when that old fisherman told us how to treat a sea urchin injury?'

Zoe shook her head.

'Don't you remember?' he urged incredulously. 'He said that if you stand on a sea urchin, their spines break off into your foot. It's

super-painful. They're apparently really difficult to get out, so you either have to get them cut out, or you have to bash your foot with something like a big glass bottle until the spines are broken up inside your foot. That way, your body has a better chance of ejecting the small bits over time.'

Looking horrified, Zoe said, 'We should probably be wearing shoes.'

Pip shrugged. It wasn't often that the children wore shoes. They didn't know then that as adults, they would look back on their carefree childhood and see that in many ways, they grew up just as wildly as the creatures around them did!

As she stood to stretch, Zoe looked down at her new T-shirt and admired the picture of palm trees silhouetted against a purple sunset. 'I like this T-shirt Mum bought me yesterday,' she said contentedly. 'Although it's a bit long.' She twisted around to look at it. Indeed, it hung past her bather bottoms.

They had been to the sleepy seaside village

of Kuta the day before to do some shopping at the beach markets. Pip and Zoe had enjoyed following the tan-coloured Balinese cows as they were walked along Kuta beach by a boy around their own age.

They'd walked down the sandy track to the beach from the markets to look at the surf thundering against the sand. It had been the middle of the day, and the sun had been beating down, bleaching the colour out of the palm trees and sand while somehow making the sea glitter a bright and brilliant blue. They'd had to squint to see it stretch into the horizon, the glare painful for their eyes.

In the afternoon, back in Sanur, their parents had hired a prahu, a fishing boat with outriggers and a bimini cover for shade. It was painted in bright blue, yellow and red which made it look jaunty and happy as it rocked on the water. The children had spent a couple of hours in the lagoon, fishing and swimming. When it had been time to go in, they sat astride the timber outriggers and hung on as the prahu picked up speed. Only Zoe had been washed off twice, much to Pip's amusement.

They still had a few more days left of their holiday before they had to go back to Jakarta for the start of the school term.

'I like it here at Sanur,' Zoe commented, looking around. 'The surf scares me at Kuta.' She looked back towards the beach, lifting her chin to the offshore wind and feeling it lift her hair off her face. The brick beach huts they were staying in were scattered along the foreshore, shaded by the palm trees. Narrow porches provided just enough room for a small bamboo table and two chairs to the side of the front door, which was heavy and wooden and had pictures of fishermen and their prahus carved into it. It hung a little wonky, so there were gaps between the door and the frame, which let the mosquitos in at night.

Zoe enjoyed the nightly ritual of dressing in long-sleeved cotton pyjamas and tucking the mosquito nets in around the beds, making sure there were no gaps. They'd lie there and listen to the waves and the crackle of the palm fronds in the wind and watch the ghostly mosquito nets billow as the ocean breeze snuck in between the cracks in the doors and windows and puffed about their room.

Standing so far out on the exposed reef, Zoe could just make out their hut by her mother's blue sarong hanging over the porch rail to dry. The waiters in the restaurant next door were starting their nightly ritual of putting tables and chairs out on the sand and lighting the lanterns hanging from bamboo poles. The sun was setting behind the palm trees, which sent fingers of shadow down the beach to the water's edge.

'The waiters at the restaurant look so small from here,' Zoe murmured.

She turned to look out to sea and realized, with a start, that they were almost at the reef drop-off, where the ocean heaved and rolled, alive against the reef, swelling to begin its reclamation of the rockpools and creatures within. They'd been so focused on exploring that they now had no idea how much time had passed. 'Pip, look how far out we are! The tide's coming in. We should start going back,' Zoe suddenly said, feeling a little worried.

'Okay,' Pip replied, not looking up. He didn't register the shift in light and tide, focused as he was on catching the darting blue fusiliers with his net.

Reasoning that they still had enough light left to keep looking whilst aiming for the beach instead of the open ocean, they went from one rockpool to the next, still not tired of the anticipation each new pool brought them. Each had a different collection of soft and hard corals, pretty shells, fish, crabs, urchins, and eels. Some had sandy bottoms, and some had grassy seaweed growing out of the sand which would sway and move as though each pool had its own currents. Some were big enough to swim in, and some were so tiny they'd fit in the palm of your hand, yet they still had their own little microcosm of creatures, corals, and sand.

A while later, Zoe looked up.

'Pip, the fishermen are coming out. We

really need to hurry,' Zoe said urgently, watching a lone fisherman walking towards them. He had a bamboo basket hanging at his back to which a lantern was tied, already lit. His tall fishing rod rested on his shoulder, the tip bowing and bobbing as he walked.

The water was rushing around their ankles now. They still had a long way to walk to get back to the beach. This was fine if they could see where they were putting their feet, but the sun was even lower behind the palm trees now, and there were long shadows in the rockpools themselves that were made more turgid by the rushing seawater filling them up. What were once fascinating ecosystems ripe for exploration now felt like dark holes full of danger and threat.

As the fisherman approached, he paused for a moment to look at the children. With concern on his face he said, '*Ayo anak- anak buru-buru, air laut lagi pasang dan semakin gelap.*' (C'mon kids, you need to hurry. The tide is coming in and it's

getting dark.)

Finally, fully aware of the risk they faced, anxiety bubbled up. Pip and Zoe thanked him and promised to hurry. Walking as fast as they could towards the beach, they waded through the rushing water.

'How did it get so dark so quickly?' Pip wondered aloud, shaking his head.

Annoyed and scared, Zoe grumbled, 'I *have* been telling you to hurry up and stop looking. I warned you that it was getting dark.'

'It's not just my fault! You were looking, too!' Pip shot back crossly.

In silence, they pressed on, concentrating hard on keeping their balance as the water rushed in and the deepening darkness concealed the cracks, crevices, and holes in the reef, conspiring to make them fall. Seized by fright, Zoe suddenly exclaimed, 'I can't see where I'm putting my feet at all now!'

Pip knew she was visualizing all the poisonous creatures they'd seen that afternoon. He was, too. Sounding braver than he felt, he said, 'Just keep going.'

It wasn't long before the water was rushing around their knees and they were inching their feet forward bit by bit, feeling their way with their toes. There was no way of knowing what was beneath them now. The beach still seemed impossibly far away, and was completely obscured by darkness. The lanterns at the restaurant guttered and swayed in the sea breeze. It felt dream-like, standing in the dark swirling water, fear of the unseen squeezing

around them tightly, while the magical lights floated in the darkness beyond.

'Just keep your eyes on the lanterns and head straight for them,' Pip eventually instructed.

'Okay,' said Zoe, her voice wavering. After a while, Zoe murmured, 'The water is so deep...' Pip could hear the panic in her voice as the dark water swelled around their hips.

'If it gets too deep, we'll just have to swim,' Pip said pragmatically.

'How will we do that with our buckets and your rod?'

'With one hand!' Pip laughed, starting to feel reckless. His laughter died away as he remembered the contents of his bucket, however. 'I still have the lionfish in the bucket!' he gasped.

'Oh my God! What if it stings us? Pour it out away from you!' Zoe shouted as she bellyflopped into the water and started swimming awkwardly, holding her now-empty bucket and net above the water and trying desperately not to let her feet touch the reef.

Pip poured out the contents of his bucket and pushed off into the water, starting the same awkward one-armed swim.

The wind had picked up by this point. Sprays of water flicked off the waves as they rolled towards the beach, and saltwater splashed into their mouths and eyes, stinging mercilessly. *At least the tide is coming in and washing us towards the shore*, Zoe thought.

The water was dark and menacing around them, but they just kept their heads up and their eyes on the lanterns.

'It doesn't feel like we're getting any closer,' Zoe shouted after some time.

'Just keep going,' Pip gasped.

Exhaustion suddenly seemed to weigh them down. A wave rolled over Zoe's head and her bucket filled with water, pulling her down. It was hard to tell which way was up. The bucket was too heavy, the metal handle digging into her fingers. Quickly realizing that she had no choice, she released the bucket and pulled thro-

-ugh the water.

Bursting through the surface and gasping for breath, she saw the stars blinking despite her stinging, bleary eyes.

'Look at the lanterns!' she heard Pip shout. He sounded far away.

Before she could respond or ask him to slow down, another wave rolled over the top of her. She sank again, her knee scraping the reef. She felt it gouge at her flesh. She was sure it was bleeding, but at least it gave her a footing. Pushing off, she tried to stand. Getting purchase, she broke the surface of the water again, her hair wet and heavy over her face. She stumbled... and another wave knocked her forward.

Her knees scraped against the rocks again. She lurched forward on her hands and knees to the shallows. Suddenly, she felt her T-shirt pull tightly around her as Pip grabbed at the fabric to pull her to safety beyond the waves. They both collapsed onto the sand, exhausted.

'We made it,' he puffed, too tired to sound

victorious.

Zoe was unable to speak. Her throat hurt, sand scratched her eyes, and her hair was a wet, sandy tangle, seaweed knotted into it. She lay on the sand, coughing.

'That was a bit scary,' Pip admitted, rubbing his eyes.

Sitting up, Zoe began to cry. 'I lost my bucket.'

Pip looked at her and managed to laugh. 'You'll get fined for littering.'

They sat in silence for a few minutes. Shivering, Zoe eventually asked, 'Aren't you cold?'

'Yup. I can't wait for a hot shower. I'm starving, too. I'm going to have two servings of nasi goreng.'

Helping each other up, they started to walk along the beach to their hut. A figure ahead, silhouetted by the lights behind, marched towards them. Pip and Zoe could tell by the curly hair that it was their mother.

'It's Mum. She's going to be *so* angry,' Zoe

sighed, echoing Pip's thoughts.

As the children braced themselves, Margie shouted, 'Where on *earth* have you two been? I've been looking everywhere for you! I was starting to get really worried. You kids can't just disappear for hours and not tell me where you're going! I thought you were going to look at the rockpools, but then I couldn't see you anywhere!'

The children hung their heads, despondent.

'Look at you both!' Margie pressed on. 'You're soaked! You can't swim in the dark! It's so dangerous. You know better than that...'

Margie suddenly stopped speaking as she noticed the children's faces for the first time.

'What happened?' she asked gently.

'Sorry, Mum,' Pip and Zoe mumbled in unison.

'We just didn't realize how far we'd walked,' Zoe continued. 'We lost track of time. It got dark so quickly, the tide came in, and we...' She trailed off as her voice started to wobble, tears in her eyes. Her knee stung, and she suddenly felt too tired to tell the whole story.

'You look exhausted,' Margie conceded. 'But this is still *really* irresponsible of you. I don't mind you exploring, but you *must* tell me how far you're going, and you *must* always come back before it gets dark!' Pulling the children towards her into a tight hug, she sighed, 'Anyway, you're here now. And you're shivering. Let's go back to the hut so you can have a hot shower and get dry. Everyone is ready for supper at the restaurant. You must be hungry.'

'Starving!' the children replied.

As she walked them to the hut, Margie asked, 'Will you be alright to meet me at the restaurant?'

'Yes, Mum. We'll be quick,' Pip nodded.

After Pip had dumped his bucket on the sand and leaned the fishing rod against the railing of the porch, he and Zoe rushed inside to get ready.

Zoe relished the pleasure of the hot water

washing the salt and sand out of her eyes and ears and tried to ignore the stinging of her cuts and grazes, instead focusing on the luxury of combing the conditioner through her hair. She turned the water as hot as she could bear and felt the heat seep into her body as she watched the seaweed clump around the plug.

Feeling fresh, relieved, and somewhat proud to have survived their latest adventure, the children dressed quickly. It felt so good to be dry.

'Are we going to tell Mum and Dad the full story?' Zoe broached hesitantly.

'I don't know. Let's decide later,' Pip said dismissively. 'All I can think about now is how much I'm going to eat for supper!'

'Me too. I. Am. Famished!' Zoe replied. 'I hope we get ice cream tonight...'

Waiting patiently beside him, Zoe watched Pip fumble with the padlock and key in the dull porch light. When it finally clicked, Pip leapt from the porch, shrieking, 'Race you!' with newfound energy. He landed off-balance in the sand before recovering and sprinting into the darkness, towards the restaurant lanterns.

'What? Wait! That's *so* not fair!' Zoe yelled, leaping into the night.

A SQUIRREL'S FLIGHT
TO FREEDOM

Chapter One

'How much *longer*?' Pip moaned as they inched through the traffic in downtown Jakarta.

'We haven't even left the city and you're already complaining!' Margie sighed, exasperated.

Pip and Zoe were already bored and bickering in the backseat, and their parents, Margie and Charles, were accordingly already irritated. As the family stopped at another busy intersection, cars and trucks ignored lanes, honked their horns, and inched dangerously close together, their rear mirrors mere centimetres from each other.

Zoe was looking at the passengers in the Toyota next to them when a necrotic hand with dirty rags half-wrapped around stumps—stumps that were once fingers, Zoe quickly realized—tapped on her window.

She started with surprise. 'Oh, Mum, Dad! There's a beggar at my window.'

Charles looked around. 'I didn't even see him coming. He must have crawled behind that Toyota beside us.'

Margie peered over. 'He looks like he has leprosy. The poor man.'

Indeed, the man had open flat wounds on his arms and legs. The skin around them looked like it was peeling and oozing. His feet were stumps, and he only had a few fingers left.

Zoe stared through the window and into his eyes, which were begging, devoid of hope, dry, and unblinking. Maybe he was blind.

'Here, Zoe. Drop this note out of the window. Only open the window a tiny bit and don't touch him. Just drop the money,' Margie instructed.

Zoe instantly felt uncomfortable with this. It felt disrespectful. But she did what she was told: she opened the window an inch, pushed the note through, and let it go. She watched the man look up at the window opening, reach up with his stumpy hand, miss the note, and then anxiously try to follow it with his eyes as it fluttered down to the road. He shuffled over to where it had landed—just by one of the back tyres—and tucked it into the front of his torn, dirty T-shirt. He looked up at Zoe's window and dipped his head in thanks.

Zoe knew he couldn't see her because of the tint on the windows, but all the same, she blushed with shame and pity.

'The lights have changed. Is he moving away?' Margie asked urgently. 'It's so dangerous for him to be crawling around in the road. Drivers can hardly see him.'

As the cars started to slowly move, the beggar shuffled to the small cement island around the traffic lights and disappeared behind the wall of cars.

'That makes me feel so sad,' Zoe said quietly, her voice trembling.

'It is sad,' Charles nodded. 'Since there's no welfare system—a government system that helps to feed and house the poor—here in Indonesia, it's important to give, if you can.'

'But you have to be careful, as begging is a big business as well, and children are often maimed so they can get more sympathy and therefore donations. It's tricky,' Margie added.

Completely confused, Zoe looked at Pip, shrugged her shoulders, and sank back into her seat so she could look at the smoggy sky instead of the grim reality of the streets around her.

After what seemed like hours of crawling through traffic, Pip complained, 'Carita beach is *miles* away!'

'Yes. It does take time,' Charles responded. 'But it's worth it. Shall we dig some heffalump traps this time?' he added, glancing at the children in the rear-view mirror.

'Yes, please!' Pip said quickly, excited at the

prospect of digging holes in the sand to try and trap the ever-elusive heffalump. Charles grinned.

They were heading west to the province of Banten. After slowly making their way through the city of Cilegon, they turned left to follow the coastal road. The busy, sprawling metropolis of Jakarta gave way to farmland. The road was mostly sealed but narrow, and only allowed for one car to travel along it at a time. They would have to slow down and move onto the sandy verge to allow any oncoming vehicles to pass.

Hours later, as the road dipped and wound through sleepy seaside towns, Zoe shouted, 'There it is!' The sea, glittering on their right, lifted them out of their torpor. 'Can we wind our windows down?'

'Please! Please!' Pip implored.

'Great idea,' Charles said, a grin on his face. They all pumped the window handles and let the salty air whip through the car.

'Woo-hoo!' yelled Pip.

'Hang on!' Charles shouted as he sped up

for the dip in the road. The children shrieked with excitement as their stomachs lurched and their bottoms lifted off the seat.

'Again! Again!' they shouted.

Happiness was settling in as they anticipated the days ahead of swimming, building sandcastles, setting heffalump traps, and climbing the beach almond trees. The last half hour of the drive felt interminable as the kids looked out for the signs to Carita Beach.

'Here we are,' said their dad with satisfaction as they turned right off the sealed road and onto a sandy track that led them to the open bamboo gates, welcoming them to the Carita Beach Huts. They bumped slowly up to reception. '*So* good to stretch the legs,' Charles moaned as he climbed out of the driver's seat of their trusty old Holden Kingswood.

After they all had clambered out and stretched, they headed up the steps to the reception — although 'reception' was a generous term for the bamboo open-air building that always had sand on the cement floor. There was a wooden desk to the left, where Margie and Charles now went to check in and collect the key to their hut. To the right was a little wood-framed glass cabinet, behind which were neatly stacked rows of packets of Chiclets chewing gum, Kretek cigarettes, lighters, matches, display bottles of Coke and 7Up, and other local crackers and sweets for sale. The sparse bamboo and cane furniture was all angled to catch the sliver of a view of the ocean through the leaves of the beach almond trees, their twisting trunks sprouting out of the sand. There was a sandy pathway in between the trees that led to the beach and the glittering water beyond.

On the wall to the left of the makeshift 'store' was a picture of several men of the Dani tribe from Irian Jaya, which always made the children point and giggle. The men wore nothing but gourds, bands of feathers around their biceps and heads, and pigs' tusks, which pierced their noses and rested against their cheeks.

'That is a picture of one of the tribes that live

in the highlands of Irian Jaya,' Charles called over to them, overhearing their giggles. The children blushed. 'They've lived like that for millennia, and have survived in very remote and unforgiving places.' Wandering over to look at the picture more closely, he registered the children's stained cheeks. Laughing, he said, 'Don't be embarrassed. It's interesting to see how humans have adapted to their environments all around the world. Indonesia itself has hundreds of different ethnicities, religions, and languages spread across this archipelago.'

'What's an archipelago?' Pip asked.

'A collection of islands making up one country. Indonesia is made up of around seventeen thousand islands. We're on the island of Java right now, and the Dani tribe live on an island east of here, which is divided into two parts. Half belongs to Indonesia and is called Irian Jaya, and the other half is called Papua New Guinea and is independent. It only became independent in the year you two were born —

1975. So only nine years ago.'

The children looked at their father quite blankly.

Charles smiled. 'Okay, I promise no more history lessons.' He held up the key. 'Let's go to the hut. It's the same one as last time. Do you remember what it's called?'

'Lima!' Zoe shouted.

'Lima number five!' Pip added, taking off after Zoe, who had already run down the sandy cement steps and along the sandy driveway toward their hut. They counted each hut until they reached the fifth one. It was about halfway down the sandy driveway, as there were only a dozen or so huts in the 'resort'.

They waited, puffing, on the narrow cement steps to the front door for their parents to bring the car down. Once they pulled up, Margie got out of the passenger seat to come and unlock the door, which was bamboo-framed and plywood locked with a latch and padlock.

The children immediately ran in to explore. Even though they'd stayed there before, they wanted to be the first to see what, if anything, had changed.

The hut had a cement slab for a floor, which sat about thirty centimetres above the sand. As they entered, the galley kitchen was to their left. It was dark and had only one lightbulb hanging from the ceiling to brighten the space. There was a cement benchtop with a small gas cooker, and on the shelf below were a few bowls, plates, glasses, and some cutlery. There was no fridge, but there was enough space on the floor to put the enormous orange, white-lidded Esky that Charles was dragging in with help from the man who'd checked them in.

Charles ordered some ice to be delivered in two days' time, when the ice in the Esky would have melted. Zoe loved to run her hand over the ice when it was delivered. It was one enormous rectangular block, too big for a child to wrap their arms around. It would be delivered dripping and strapped to a two-wheeled trolley, and after pulling it into the kitchen, the man who had delivered it would get out his chisel a-

-nd hammer it into chunks. He'd then put them in the Esky after wiping off the sand and bits of dirt. It was mesmerising watching him reduce that huge block of ice into a shattered mess that would keep their food cold for a few more days.

Next to the kitchen was the bathroom. It also only had one lightbulb hanging from an electric cord hooked to the ceiling to give enough light to navigate your way past the bak mandi and towards the loo.

The bak mandi was a cement square tub filled with cool water. There was a single tap on the wall to replenish it with, and a small round bucket with a rounded handle to the side. You used this bucket to dip into the bak mandi, scoop up some water, and then pour over yourself to wash.

'This bak mandi is fish-free!' Pip exclaimed excitedly. 'Do you remember that one that had fish in it to eat the mosquito larvae?'

'I do, but I can't remember where it was,' Zoe pondered. Then, she said, 'Let's check out my room!'

They skipped up the three cement steps that led to the bedroom next door to the bathroom. It was small, but to Zoe's eye, it was wonderful. 'I love this room,' she sighed. There was a double bed pushed into the corner, and there somehow wasn't a single crease in the tightly tucked sheets. There were two pillows neatly laid side by side, and the timber framework of the hut was exposed and doubled as narrow shelving around the room. There were also built-in plywood shelves in the corner to the right of the door, where Zoe already knew she would neatly organise her clothes. At the end of the bed was a small bamboo table with mosquito coils and matches on it at the ready, and another small bamboo table with a lamp on it had been nestled beside the bed comfortingly. Above the bed on the far wall was a timber-framed bamboo window which opened outwards over the sandy driveway with a view to the mountainous jungle beyond.

There was no glass in the window frames. In fact, the walls of the entire hut were made of bamboo matting. The walls billowed slightly in the wind, the onshore breezes constantly seeping through the cracks, keeping the room cool.

'I'm in the room next door,' Pip announced, running out to inspect it. Their parents would be in the bedroom on the other side of the living space, which was almost entirely taken up by a long wooden table and bamboo chairs. Two low wicker chairs with cushions on either side of a small glass-topped bamboo table were tucked into the corner between Zoe and Pip's bedrooms — perfect for playing cards or reclining with drinks.

The living space was completely open. Instead of a wall and doors, there was a wall of large waxy pale green leaves, completely shielding the hut from the sun. The trunks and branches of the beach almond trees had grown into each other so that the canopy reached all the way down to the sand, creating a dome of lovely luminescent shade. The leaves shifted with the onshore breezes and constantly drifted to the ground.

But best of all, hanging from the hut frame and tucked just under the eaves of the thatched roof were two wicker hanging egg chairs.

'Get in!' Pip cried.

She didn't need to be told twice. Zoe climbed into the closest egg chair, gripped the sides of it with her hands, and pushed her feet into frame. 'I'm ready!'

Pip turned the chair until the rope was tightly twisted before letting it go. It spun dizzyingly back into place. The world spun into

a blur as Zoe shrieked, pushing harder with her feet and gripping tighter with her hands to stop her limbs from flying out. If you left your mouth open, saliva would stream out, impossible to avoid when you were laughing.

'Okay, my turn,' Pip said as Zoe unfurled her legs and stood unsteadily.

'Alright, kids, come and help bring in the bags, please!' Margie called.

After a resounding groan, Pip and Zoe tottered giddily across the room to go the car.

'Can we have a look at the beach now?' Zoe asked once the bags had all been brought in.

'That's fine,' Charles said, 'but please drag out the beach chairs so that you can find your way back.'

Filled with excitement, the twins walked down the sandy path that led through the trees, dragging a bamboo beach chair each. Ducking through the branches, they stepped out into the bright sunshine, blinking and squinting.

The bay curved to the left and right, and they could see that the fishing boats were moored close to shore. The waves lapped gently against the sand, and the sky was clear and blue. They could make out the volcano, Anak Krakatoa, on the horizon, white smoke climbing in a twisted pillar above it.

Chapter Two

Pip and Zoe spent the next few days swimming, fishing, and digging heffalump traps in the sand.

'What do heffalumps look like again, Dad?' Pip inquired.

'Well, they have four legs and dark fur like a platypus,' Charles said, a glint in his eye. 'They have flat noses, and they walk along the bottom of the sea eating seaweed. At night-time, they walk out of the waves and up the beach to forage for crabs. So if you dig a hole deep enough and put some cornflakes in it, one might fall in and get stuck there because their legs are very short.' He leaned into the children conspiringly. 'They're extremely shy, and very, very rare. I've only ever seen one once.'

'You *have*?' the twins gasped in unison.

Charles looked at them and nodded his head very seriously. 'It was very late one night, and the moon was full. I came down to the beach and was standing just over there.' The children looked to where he was pointing. 'I noticed something dark and roundish. It sort of rolled as it emerged from the waves. I couldn't believe it when it wombled out of the water and walked slowly on its short legs, scavenging for crabs along the water's edge.

'I watched it for a while and kept very still. But unfortunately, a mosquito was biting my arm, so I had to scratch, and that was enough to scare the heffalump. It wombled back into the waves as quickly as it could and disappeared below the surface.'

Pip and Zoe stared at him suspiciously.

'What? You don't believe me?' Charles asked, wide-eyed. 'Keep digging your heffalump traps in the sand and you'll see.'

Indeed, their incredulity wasn't enough to stop Pip and Zoe from doing just that every night, and, sure, enough, each morning, the cornflakes were gone and replaced with footprints. It took hours of close examination and debate to try and determine what it was that had eaten the cornflakes at the bottom of the pit.

That came later, though. For now, bored of fishing, Pip and Zoe spent the afternoon floating on the waves, legs dangling over the edge of the tractor tyre inner tubes they'd brought with them until a surprise set of waves tipped them off and into the white wash, filling every orifice with sand. Spluttering as they surfaced, they decided to head back to the hut.

Later that day, as Pip and Zoe relaxed in the welcome shade after spending so much time in the heat of the day, an old fisherman called through the trees: '*Ikan! Ikan!*' (Fish! Fish!)

'*Silakan masuk Pak,*' Charles replied. (Come in.)

The old man bowed his head and walked sideways through the branches of the trees, balancing the baskets on the ends of the long pole resting across his shoulders. He plonked himself on the sand in front of the hut, resting the baskets beside him, relieved of the weight. In the baskets were several fish he'd caught that morning.

'Those ones look good, don't you think, Charles?' Margie said, pointing at the red-gold snapper, which still gleamed, freshly caught as it was. Margie negotiated a price and asked the

fisherman to prepare them for her in stumbling Indonesian: '*Tolong mempersiapkan ikan itu Pak?*' (Please could you prepare the fish for us?) Nodding and smiling, the fisherman began to prepare the fish, and as Zoe watched, she noticed that his eyes looked slightly bleached from overexposure to the reflection of the sun off the sea.

The fisherman proceeded to scale the fish, scraping his sharp knife against the scales at an angle. Pip and Zoe watched in fascination. The translucent scales flicked off into the air, glinting dazzlingly in the light.

'Nothing like freshly caught fish,' Charles said later that day over his supper of fish, vegetables, steamed rice, and sambal.

Pip and Zoe weren't so convinced. 'I don't like all the bones,' Zoe mumbled uncertainly, pushing the food around her plate.

'But the tomato sauce is good with it,' Pip told her.

Still, they ate hungrily, filling up on rice.

After supper, they sat on the beach to watch the sunset. It had been a clear day, so they could just make out the puffing volcano on the horizon. Anak Krakatoa, or Krakatoa's child, was the heart of Krakatoa; it puffed and grew a meter each year since its eruption one hundred years before.

Margie and Charles reclined in their beach chairs, their drinks clinking with ice and lime and happily watching the children build their sandcastles.

'Mum, why did we celebrate the hundred-year anniversary of the eruption of Krakatoa when it caused tidal waves that killed so many people?' Zoe asked suddenly, patting out the sand from her bucket. She leaned back so she could admire the perfect castle she'd built.

'I don't really know, actually,' Margie shrugged noncommittally.

Charles had something to say however, and began: 'The Ujung Kulon National Park used to be farmed land, but was wiped out by the tsunami that was caused by Krakatoa erupting.

People didn't want to return, so the jungle was left to regenerate over the last hundred years, and in doing so has become one of the world's best national parks. And that's where the last of the Javan rhinos live. Imagine! Rhinos in Indonesia!'

'Can we go there one day?' Pip asked, always hungry for adventure.

'One day.'

'I'm afraid of Anak Krakatoa erupting and causing a tsunami here,' Zoe said, frowning and not looking up from her sandcastle, which she was patting down.

'Oh, honey, Anak Krakatoa is so small that it'll be decades before that will become a risk,' Margie responded, not really knowing if this was true or not. And, indeed, her reassurances weren't enough to stop Zoe from worrying when she lay in bed at night. She lay there listening to the waves, counting the seconds between the sighs and crashes. With her body tensed, she would hold her breath whenever the silences were long, believing that the water was being sucked out into a growing tsunami that would wash them all away. She'd breathe out with each breaking wave, relief and fatigue intermingling, until she fell asleep.

The next day, Pip and Zoe wandered to the shop in the reception to buy some Chiclets chewing gum. As usual, they only wore their bathers, and *never* any shoes.

Kicking along the sandy track and happily comparing the bubbles they could blow with their gum, they decided to climb the rickety bamboo fence to see if they could see over the top to the jungle. Impressively, Pip hooked his toes into the cross-strips of bamboo and had his chin over the top of the vertical poles in no time.

'C'mon Zoe, you can do it!' he called through gritted teeth.

Zoe couldn't get a toehold and kept slipping down the face of the fence. She tried again, clenching her teeth, and, to her delight, managed to get most of the way to the top… when her foot slipped.

Sliding down the fence, a crooked rusty nail pierced into her thigh. Sucking in her breath and tears brimming in her eyes, she moaned, 'There's a *nail* in my leg!'

Pip pushed off from the fence and leapt to the sand, making the fence wobble and teeter. 'Let me have a look,' he demanded. He recoiled as soon as he saw. 'Ooh, looks *nasty*!' He bent over and peered at the front of Zoe's thigh. 'Let's get back to the hut and show Mum.'

He let Zoe lean on him as she sniffled, trying to be brave, and hobbled along.

'*Mum!*' Pip yelled as they entered the hut. 'Zoe has a nail in her leg!'

Margie frowned as she looked up from her game of solitaire. Her brow knitted. 'Oh, that's no good. Let me have a look.'

Now in the care of her mother, Zoe's tears began to flow. Margie guided Zoe to the front of the hut so she could use the sunshine to better see what she was dealing with.

Firmly lodged in the front of Zoe's thigh was a rusty nail. No doubt about it. 'Oh dear,' she grimaced. 'I'm going to have to try to get that out. It's lucky you've had your tetanus shot.'

'It really hurts, Mum,' Zoe forced out through gritted teeth and teary eyes.

'I'm sure it does.' Margie grabbed her first aid kit and rummaged for the tweezers. 'Okay, just hold still for a sec...'

Zoe braced herself for the sting and jumped half out of her skin when her mother seized the nail and tried to pull it out. '*Arghh*! That hurts! Don't touch it!'

Margie contemplated her daughter for a minute. 'Hmm. Maybe go and have a swim in the sea. The water might soften your skin and wash it out.'

'Okay, Mum,' Zoe said uncertainly. 'I'll try.'

Zoe hobbled down to the water's edge and let the seawater wash over her legs. Still grimacing, she bent over and inspected the nail. It certainly didn't look like it was going anywhere. It was lodged in deep.

After a while, her mother called her back to the hut. Charles and Mr. Thompson, who was staying in the hut next door, were both there.

'Give us a look at the war wound, then,' Charles said jokingly.

Zoe obligingly lifted her leg so her dad and Mr. Thompson could have a look.

'Wow. Pretty impressive,' Charles remarked. 'How are you going to get it out?'

'I don't know,' Zoe said glumly.

'Come and lie down on your bed so we can have a proper look. I need to put some disinfectant on it,' Margie cut in, business as usual.

'Don't touch it, will you?' Zoe said quickly, panicked and wide-eyed.

'I promise. I'm just going to look and put

some betadine on it.'

Before laying down, Zoe wondered why her dad and Mr. Thompson had needed to come. She reasoned that they must have just wanted to see for themselves, it being a pretty impressive wound and all.

She lay back gingerly, holding her thigh. It was really starting to throb.

'Alright, darling heart, just lie still for me,' Margie soothed.

Margie gave Charles and Mr. Thompson a wary look—and suddenly, her father was wrapping himself around Zoe in a big bear hug and Mr. Thompson was laying across her legs. Zoe screamed and kicked, trying to fight them off, but she was no match for the two men.

With a look of fierce concentration, Margie leaned over Zoe's leg with the tweezers.

Zoe screamed and screamed and tried to kick again. 'You're hurting me! *You're hurting me!*' she yelped, hot tears streaming down her face and her throat dry.

'*Got it!*' Margie announced, triumphantly

holding up an inch-long crooked rusted nail.

'Wow! No wonder it wouldn't come out,' Charles said, finally loosening his grip and kissing the still-trembling Zoe on the forehead. 'You're very strong, missy. I could barely hold you!' He paused and noticed, with a pang, Zoe's horror-stricken expression. 'I'm so sorry we had to do that, but there was no other way. There are no hospitals or clinics near here, and we wouldn't be back in Jakarta for hours. It had to come out. My brave girl...' He pulled Zoe to him for a hug, rubbing her arm as she cried into his chest.

'Well, that was a bloody good show,' Mr. Thompson jested. 'Your dad's right, you're one strong girl. Lucky your mum here is a nurse. That's a pretty comprehensive first aid kit right there.'

'There's no way I'd travel anywhere without it,' Margie shrugged, laying out saline wash, disinfectant, gauze, and a bandage. 'Do you guys remember the last time we were here and that little boy who was staying next door ran up to the firecracker? He thought it wasn't working and just as he grabbed it, it exploded.'

Zoe nodded, feeling more nauseous than before. She'd never forget going with her mother to help them; the dim light in the hut next door and the boy writhing in pain on his bed with burns all across his chest, arms, and face. Margie had taken her first aid kit and given the boy pain relief and administered burn cream, leaving the tube with his mother to apply as needed. '*Jangan menggunkan kecap*, okay?' Margie had said gently. (Don't use soy sauce.)

It was widely believed that soy sauce soothed burns and prevented them from blistering. Some people still swear by this remedy.

That poor family had been waiting anxiously for their driver to return from Jakarta to take them back to the hospital. Zoe felt so sorry for the fact that the poor boy had had to wait so long. She now imagined the long, painful drive back to Jakarta and winced.

Margie had sat with the boy's mother by his

bedside, helping tend to him through the night until their car arrived.

The next day, Pip and Zoe had sat through a lecture from their parents about the danger of firecrackers with wide eyes and their full attention. It was possible then to buy firecrackers off the street corner and to light them in your own backyard, and after this terrible event, the children were banned from ever doing so.

'Zoe, have a look at that hole in your thigh before I bandage it,' Margie laughed now. 'It's pretty impressive!'

Zoe peered at the hole in her thigh that the nail left. 'It isn't bleeding as much as I thought it would,' she said.

'Yes, it's a funny thing. It must have missed your blood vessels. Let's wash it out, get the antiseptic on it, and bandage it up. We'll have to see if you need a tetanus booster when we get home. And I'm afraid that I don't think it's a good idea to swim for a while.'

'Oh *no*!' Zoe cried, suddenly feeling very

sorry for herself indeed.

'I'm sure you'll find lots of other things to do, my darling,' Margie said, and kissed Zoe on the forehead.

Chapter Three

The next day, with swimming off the agenda because of Zoe's nail injury, Pip and Zoe had spent the morning entertaining themselves in the hut. Bored of card games and swinging in the bamboo pod chairs, they decided to climb the beach almond trees. Zoe felt quite agile despite her aching thigh. As they reached and climbed from branch to branch, they found that they had passed along the front of all the huts and suddenly, it seemed, arrived in front of reception.

'Look over there,' Pip called over his shoulder.

Peering through the foliage, Zoe saw a man holding the end of a piece of fishing line, at the other end of which was tied a squirrel.

The children scurried over and asked the man, '*Boleh lihat?*' (Can we see?)

'*Iyah, boleh,*' he responded. (Yes, you can.)

'It's so cute!' Zoe breathed as she stroked the terrified little squirrel. The squirrel was sitting upright on its hind legs, and had large black eyes and great, big, pointed ears. Its red bottle brushtail stood up, stiff and twitching,

and its fur faded from a reddish brown to almost yellow on its stomach.

'Can you see how it looks as though it has loose skin on either side of its belly, between its front and back legs?' Pip asked.

'Yup, I can see.'

'Well, it uses that skin like little wings to help it glide through the air when it jumps from tree to tree,' he said importantly. 'They stick their arms and legs out, which stretches the skin out to catch the air. They can travel quite far.'

'What cool little creatures!' Zoe said. 'A flying squirrel!'

'I think that's what they're called, actually. A Javanese flying squirrel. They're related to the Australian sugar glider, I think.'

Zoe smiled. 'That's so cool. I feel so sorry for it, though. Can you see how the fishing line around its neck has rubbed the fur off and made the skin red raw?'

'Yes. I saw that already,' Pip nodded with a grimace. 'It's like a noose around its neck. The slipknot lets the noose pull tight when the squirrel tries to get away and loosens when it stops pulling. Looks like it's been trying hard to get away.'

The children watched the squirrel clamber up the tree, only to be yanked back by the neck again. Zoe winced. Pip's hypothesis was right.

Pip asked the man why he had the fishing line around the squirrel's neck, and he explained that without it, it would escape. He'd caught it in the forest and was planning on selling it. He offered it to Pip and Zoe for ten thousand rupiah, the equivalent of about ten Australian dollars at the time.

'How much do you have left of your pocket money?' Pip asked Zoe.

'I think only four thousand rupiah,' Zoe replied disappointedly. 'Not enough to buy the squirrel.' She thought back to the chewing gum she'd bought with it with regret. 'Anyway, I don't want to pay for the squirrel because I don't think it should have been caught in the first place,' she asserted.

Pip gave his sister a strange look. 'Well, we

could help it escape.'

Zoe's eyes widened. 'What are you talking about?'

It was lucky the man who owned the squirrel didn't speak English. It meant Pip and Zoe could speak freely about their hatching plan. Plus, he was leaning back in his plastic chair and talking animatedly to the man who had served them at reception days before, so he clearly wasn't paying much attention to the children.

'Can you see that it's a slipknot?' Pip asked.

'I think so.' Zoe suddenly felt nervous.

'So, the noose around the squirrel's neck loosens when there's no tension. But when there *is* tension from the fishing line, the noose tightens.'

'Okay…'

'So, if we can loosen the noose enough to slip it over the squirrel's head without the man seeing, it will escape up the tree.' Pip had a mischievous glint in his eye.

'But then what? We'll get into trouble.' Zoe

glanced guiltily at the man, who was still tipping his chair onto its back legs, blowing a cloud of pungent cigarette smoke into the air and laughing at something the other man had said.

'We could just say the squirrel escaped himself. Pretend we had nothing to do with it. But we'd better hurry. I think he's getting suspicious.'

Her heart pounding, Zoe couldn't decide what to do. She hated breaking the rules and hated getting in trouble even more, but the injustice of that poor squirrel practically hanging itself every time it tried to get away was too much.

Pip could see her waver and acted before she could try and talk him out of it. He turned his back to the man to block his view of the squirrel and bent forward. He started to loosen the slipknot, and within seconds, the noose slipped over the squirrel's head.

The squirrel didn't move for a second, not realizing it was free.

Zoe instinctively picked up the squirrel with one hand, stepped on the low bough that they'd been sitting on, and grabbed for the highest branch she could reach with her free hand. She relaxed her grasp and whispered urgently, 'Go, squirrel, go!'

In that moment, the man realized what the children had done. There was no pretending that it was an accident. He shouted out in rage, *'Astaga! Kamu lagi apain?'* (What are you doing?) He tried to leap out of his chair, but the combination of him carelessly balancing it on its hind legs and the uneven sand made him tip backwards, forcing him to involuntarily kick his legs up and shoot an arm out for balance before falling onto the sand.

Pip and Zoe looked at each other in shock and fear. 'Run,' Pip mouthed. And so, like racehorses out of the gate, Pip and Zoe bolted. But just before ducking through the trees onto the open beach, Zoe glanced back. The squirrel had wasted no time in scampering straight up the branch and leaping to the next one, safely out of reach of its captor.

The man tripped in the sand in his confusion, not knowing whether to chase the squirrel or the children.

Zoe didn't wait to find out what he'd decide to do.

The twins ran along the hot sand for a short distance before ducking back into the trees, clambering through the branches in front of other occupied huts (disturbing a couple having lunch and a woman reading a book in the process), running down the side of the fourth hut, dashing from one parked car to the next, and darting behind bins, feeling like ninjas.

'Oh, my leg hurts,' Zoe moaned. The adrenaline of the escape had masked the pain while they'd been running, but now that they were sat panting, the pain flooded through her. 'I can't believe we just did that. Do you think he'll find us?'

'Nah,' said Pip flippantly. But Zoe could tell he was just as shocked and worried. Even still, she took his feigned confidence as reassurance.

They sat there waiting for a while. When nothing happened and silence settled around them, they allowed themselves to be comforted by the fact that they'd outrun the squirrel man... and that they had achieved one of the greatest rescues of all time, of course.

Pip and Zoe had just settled into a game of Uno later that afternoon when there was a knock at the hut door. Charles, wearing only his swimming trunks, went to answer it.

The twins shot each other a look for a second before craning their necks to see who it was. They realized at the same time, that it was the squirrel man.

Zoe let out a small gasp.

The twins both instinctively recoiled and shrank into their chairs, lifting their hands of cards in front of their faces. They couldn't hear what was being said, but Zoe saw the man pointing at them. Charles turned to look at the children, his face dark and his brow knitted. He didn't say anything to them and headed back inside to get some money, ignoring them as he passed.

Pip and Zoe shrank even further into their chairs, fearing the worst. Pip looked at Zoe and mouthed the worst swear word he knew.

Zoe saw Charles give the squirrel man ten thousand rupiah, pat him on the shoulder, and say, *'Maaf mas, maaf.'* (Sorry.)

Mollified, the squirrel man bade Charles goodnight and left.

Pip and Zoe braced themselves.

Charles stalked over and said darkly, 'I'll give you one chance to explain yourselves, and it had better be good.'

Hardly able to believe their luck at being given a chance to explain, they both started talking at the same time.

'He was being really cruel to the squirrel. There was a noose made of fishing line —'

'It was rubbed red raw around the squirrel's neck —'

'It was bleeding in places —'

'He kept yanking the squirrel back by the neck —'

'The squirrel needed to be freed —'

'That man is a bad man, Daddy!'

'Alright, alright! One at a time!' Charles cut in.

Pip and Zoe took a deep breath and together explained how they felt seeing that poor squirrel being treated badly, and that they had decided in that moment to free the poor thing.

Charles interrupted them. 'Okay, I understand why you did what you did. But you need to understand that, in effect, you stole from that man.'

Pip and Zoe felt the sting and shame of those words sink in.

'He had caught the squirrel himself and was going to make some money that would help him out,' Charles continued firmly. 'If you weren't so lucky and didn't know where your next meal was coming from, you'd probably do the same thing.'

'I would *not*,' Zoe huffed indignantly. 'I wouldn't be cruel to an animal unnecessarily.'

'Okay, you've made your point,' Charles

sighed. 'I'm proud that you both care so much about treating animals humanely, but you also have to consider why people do what they do, and you can't just steal their livelihoods, which is essentially what you did. Can you both promise me that you won't do such a thing again?'

Pip and Zoe both nodded. 'Sorry, Dad. We promise,' Zoe murmured.

'Alright, then. As you were.' And with that, Charles rose, ruffled Pip's hair, and went to find Margie.

Feeling chastened, Zoe looked at Pip and said, 'I feel guilty now. Don't you?'

'Nope. I'd do it again. I have no regrets at all.' He picked up his cards. 'Your turn.'

JEMIMA THE GIBBON

Chapter One

As the shouts and clamour of the market enveloped them, Zoe instinctively reached for her father's hand, noticing Pip do the same with their mother's. Lifting the hem of her T-shirt to her nose, Zoe tried, in vain, to block the stench of wild animals. There were over two hundred stalls jammed together in the old, rundown building.

'What are these markets called again, Dad?' Zoe asked her father, Charles, as they climbed the stairs to the entrance of the building.

Puffing with exertion, Charles explained, 'The Pramuka Market. It's Southeast Asia's largest bird and wildlife market. The animals have mostly been captured in the jungles and forests, and many of them are protected species. They're sold cheaply to people who think that owning them will show that they are rich. It gives people a sense of prestige.' A flicker of sadness flashed across his face. 'Many thousands of the animals die soon after they're bought because they're not cared for properly. This keeps the demand high and the markets thriving, as it means people need to replace their deceased birds and animals regularly.' Charles glanced at his daughter, who was wide-eyed. 'Tragically, this practice is emptying the jungles and forests of Indonesia of so much of its beautiful wildlife.'

'We need to write to President Suharto about this!' exclaimed Zoe, a horrified look on her face.

Used to his daughter's outrage at injustice, he patiently replied, 'We can write and object, but the best way to stop something bad is to not support it. If people didn't buy these animals, t-

-here wouldn't be a market for them. And ideally, there would be regulations and fines for selling wild animals, too.' He shrugged. 'I just wanted you kids to see this place for yourselves, in the hopes that you'll learn something.'

As they strolled the aisles, crouching to peer into baskets and bamboo cages, they saw civets, owls, leopard cats, slow lorises, lizards, snakes, and macaques.

'Apparently, Javan tigers, orangutans, and sun bears have been seen for sale at these markets, too,' Charles said after a few minutes, shaking his head with dismay.

Up ahead, Margie had stopped at a ramshackle stall. She was reaching out to something. Skipping along to join her, the old man who owned the stall greeted the children with a toothless grin. He wore a peci on his head, a brown batik sarong and a white T-shirt. He sat among the grass baskets of ducklings and chicks, fighting roosters, kingfishers, and other jungle songbirds, all of which were for sale. Precariously stacked towers of baskets and cages rose like a metropolis around him, a thousand frightened eyes peering out.

In the midst of the stacked baskets was one pair of shining dark eyes that had stopped Margie in her tracks. Charles and the children gathered around her to stare back at the monkey, who was crouching fearfully in her too-small cage.

'She's injured. She has no chance,' Margie said quietly, her voice breaking slightly.

The old man explained that the monkey's mother had been trapped and killed in the jungles of Java, and the baby's foot had been caught in the snare. He'd bought her from a hunter only a week before.

'I feel terrible for her. She won't sell with that injury. She'll die,' Margie said sadly.

'We can't do anything about it,' Charles responded compassionately but firmly. 'It's beyond our control. We can't buy her. It would just support the illegal trade of animals.'

'But we could take her to the zoo. Don't they have a primate rehabilitation program at the zoo?'

Zoe had seen her dad waver in the beams of her mother's hazel eyed gaze before. He glanced at the baby monkey, who was still cowering from the noise and glare.

'Please, Charles,' Margie implored. 'The poor thing… I really think it's the right thing to do.'

'Daddy, we can't leave her!' the children added. 'She looks so frightened… Please can we rescue her, Dad? Please?'

Hesitating, Charles looked at his children's expectant faces. Shaking his head, he sighed, 'I can't believe I'm doing this.' He reached for is wallet. 'This goes against everything I've tried to teach you today…'

The children watched, agape, as their father negotiated a price. Margie meanwhile pressed her lips together, trying not to smile.

Charles seemed to have enough money in his wallet to pay the old man a satisfactory amount. Zoe thought that either the monkey was very cheap, or her father must be very rich.

The old man smiled and handed Margie the bamboo cage, the tiny monkey gripping the rails within. He gave the children three sugar bananas for the journey. *'Untuk monyet, bukan untuk kalian,'* he laughed. (For the monkey, not you.)

In the car, the children shrank against the car doors in surprise, squealing. The baby monkey, wriggling free from their mother's grasp, had leapt onto the backseat between them, dropped to the floor, and scrambled into the cavity under the driver's seat. Their father staunchly kept his feet on the pedals and his eyes on the road.

'Gosh, that gave me a fright!' said Zoe.

'Me too!' Pip agreed.

'And me!' added Margie.

'I hope she doesn't bite me on the leg,' remarked Charles, nervously adjusting his posture. In an attempt to reassure the baby monkey, Margie had unwisely taken her out of her small bamboo cage. Barely concealing his disapproval, Charles pointed out, 'You probably shouldn't have taken her out of her cage.'

Margie bit her lip sheepishly. 'Yes, probably not. Sorry. I just thought I could reassure her…' Her voice trailed away.

'What do we do now?' Pip asked of no one in particular.

Turning to face the children, Margie passed a sugar banana to Pip, the older of the twins by three minutes. 'Just offer her this,' Margie instructed. 'Don't try and get her out. If she's feeling safe enough, she'll take it.'

Zoe noticed her father shake his head slightly. 'Who buys a baby monkey?' he muttered under his breath.

Hanging their heads upside down, Pip and Zoe peered with curiosity at the terrified baby monkey. She was so tiny and malnourished. Her round black eyes glistened in the shadows. She bared her teeth in self-defence.

'You'll be alright, little monkey,' Zoe whispered in pity.

Reaching down, Pip held the banana in

front of the cowering monkey and waited. After several long minutes, a little dark leathery hand reached out and snatched it.

Zoe giggled. 'You flinched!'

'Did *not*,' Pip scowled.

The monkey's arm had a thin covering of light grey fur that stood on end. The children watched her eat quickly and hungrily, pushing the banana into her mouth until her cheeks were so round and full of squashed banana that she could barely chew.

Feeling slightly sick from being upside down for most of the journey, Zoe was relieved when they arrived home. Hariyanto, their new gardener, opened the tall black metal gates upon their arrival.

It was always a relief to drive into the oasis of their garden after being in the chaos of the city. Tall hedges along the fence line gave them seclusion — and a winning place to hide between the fence and hedge in games of hide-and-seek, so long as you weren't afraid of the rats and snakes that lurked there! An old mango tree shaded an entire corner, frangipani trees dotted the lawn, and a large, pale-green-leafed cassia tree shaded the pond to the right of the driveway. The two-story house had a gabled roof and casement windows that opened charmingly onto the tropical garden, which wrapped around three sides of the rectangular building.

The building was typical of the houses in that suburb of South Jakarta, built after the second world war. It was the last residential area to be developed by the Dutch colonial administration before Indonesia claimed its independence.

Zoe loved the way the casement windows opened outwards to the garden, inviting you to lean on the sills; to gaze out and dream. Each windowpane had black wrought iron security bars in a pretty diamond pattern fixed into the black painted timber frames, which contrasted elegantly against the white walls. The windows on the second floor were interrupted by a small veranda, which was enclosed by white curlicued metal railings and was only accessible via the guestroom.

Airy and cool inside, the ceilings soared, and the concrete walls made the house feel solid and safe. It seemed to Zoe that the whole house wrapped itself around one huge Roman Doric pillar on the corner of the grand staircase. She loved to sit on the bottom step and lean against that pillar, tracing the grooves with her fingers. She'd look up to contemplate how it seemed to grow into the ceiling, tree-like, and to admire the fluted and scalloped light fitting that cupped the ceiling and glowed prettily at night.

The entire living area wrapped in an L-shape around the staircase. The piano was against the low wall, which flanked the first landing of the wide staircase. That landing was the perfect place to spy on the glamorous parties their parents held, the enormous potted palm providing jungle camouflage. The children would crouch behind the pot and peep between the fronds at the guests milling about; at the elegant women drinking champagne in flat round glasses; at the men punctuating the air with their cigarettes, accentuating their stories. The glowing ends of the cigarettes looked like fireflies in the low-lit room and the smoke curled through the crowd, puffed into the air by lifted chins. The smoke gave the scene an ethereality that Zoe loved.

Zoe always admired her mother's beauty on nights like that: her bronzed, bare shoulders; her silk halter neck tops; her flowing skirts; her gold strappy kitten heels. Before the night's festivities, she would help her mother prepare by carefully clasping the dainty buckles on her shoes, and in reward, her mother would stamp a gold powder love heart on her cheek. Zoe would always take this close proximity as an opportunity to gaze at the barely visible gold hearts and stars stamped across her mother's décolletage; her bold gold earrings; her shiny coloured lips; the kohl lining her hazel eyes; her eyelashes, heavy with mascara; her gold-brown curls, soft around her face. She was always the belle of the ball. Stood beside her father, who w-

-as broad-shouldered and an imposing six-foot-three in a white jacket tuxedo, with dark hair and brooding good looks, they made quite the pair.

They greeted their guests with charm, and the children would watch, fascinated, as the conviviality rose in a slow crescendo with each minute that passed by.

At one such party, Hariyanto had been dressed in dark trousers and a starched batik shirt. His back was straight, and he was handing out clinking drinks, fizzing champagne, and hors d'oeuvres. He had looked *uncomfortable* in his formal clothing. Spotting the children hiding, he'd frowned at them and then, with a twinkle in his eye, made a funny face, making them laugh. Later, standing with his back to the staircase railing, he'd passed them a miniature vol-au-vent each to snack on. Giggling, Zoe had whispered through the palm fronds, '*Kamu kelihatan ganteng dong.*' (You look handsome.)

Pip had screwed up has face and punched her in the arm while Hariyanto feigned insult.

Trying not to laugh, he playfully scolded her for teasing him.

When the party had streamed through to the dining room for the buffet dinner, the children had snuck upstairs to bed, thrilled with the success of not having been spotted by their parents or the guests… or so they thought! They had been completely unaware that the hiding children, identifiable by their giggles, had become a talking point for the evening.

The mahogany writing desk on the opposite wall to the piano had a retractable roller top and two dial phones on it. Zoe loved to curl up on her father's lap while he made his endless business calls, ear to his chest, comforted by the baritone rumble of his voice. Meanwhile, the swimming pool would glitter through the windows to the left, the deep patio stretched along the bottom of the L, accessible through a multitude of glass French doors. A long, draping jungle vine hung from the patio roof, perfect for swinging, Tarzan-like, when their parents weren't looking. Past the staircase and through an arch was the dining room with walls painted dark red, and beyond that was the kitchen and garage.

It was here, in the garage, that the old Kingswood now pulled to a halt. The children, bursting with excitement, could barely wait for the car to stop so that they could declare the news of the strange animal in their car to Hariayanto and Ibu Marsi, their nanny.

'How will we get the monkey out?' Pip asked, shuffling along the backseat with his feet up so as not to scare her.

'Not sure, but let's close the garage door,' Charles responded.

Ibu Marsi pushed the swinging kitchen door open just enough to lean through and summon the children to supper, unaware that, for the time being, supper was the last thing on their minds.

'*Ada monyet di dalam mobil!*' (There's a monkey in the car!) the twins shouted, jittery with anticipation.

'*Wah, astaga!*' she replied, surprise and

disapproval sweeping across her face.

Ears straining, Pip and Zoe listened to the adults discussing the plan of action. Hariyanto and their mother climbed into the car, each armed with a towel, and closed the doors behind them.

'Why do they need the towels, Dad?' Pip asked, frowning.

'They're going to try and pull the monkey out gently, but because she's stressed and frightened, she may bite. The towel will stop it from hurting. She only has baby teeth, though, so even if she does bite, it won't do much damage.'

Even when standing on her tiptoes and tilting her chin as much as she could, all Zoe could see through the car windows was Hariyanto's shoulder, his arm stretched down, and the flank of her mother's hip as she kneeled on the backseat and reached for the monkey.

Quite suddenly, Margie sat back in the seat, her brown curls falling in her eyes and her face flushed.

And there, clinging to her chest, was the baby monkey.

Pip rushed to open the door.

Holding the towel across the monkey's back, Margie inched out of the car. The monkey looked so tiny in Margie's arms, her eyes wild with terror. Carefully, they placed the monkey back in its cage, where it would stay until they took her to the zoo the next morning.

Chapter Two

'What happened?' Margie asked with surprise as she eyed the monkey, still in the cage. Charles had just returned from the zoo, looking regretful.

'Turns out the primate rehabilitation centre is at capacity. They've asked us to take care of her until she's bigger and to cover the veterinary costs for the repair of her foot,' he sighed. 'I did learn that she's a Javan silvery gibbon, though, not a monkey. They're only found in Java and, surprise, surprise, they're endangered.'

And just like that, a baby Javan silvery gibbon became a part of the family! They named her Jemima. Over the next few weeks, Jemima grew accustomed to her human family. She clung to whoever was caring for her, and Margie would wrap Jemima to her with a sarong in the traditional Indonesian way of carrying babies.

Slowly but surely, the fear faded from Jemima's eyes.

'How old do you think she is?' asked Pip one day.

'She's probably about a year old,' Margie responded. 'I think that when they're born, they don't have any hair except a little tuft on their heads. They're also nursed – you know, they drink their mother's milk, like human babies do – for about a year. The fact that she's eating fruit and has fur means that she's at least a year old, which will help her survival.'

As Jemima grew, she interacted with her human family more and more. She happily wrapped her long arms and legs around the necks and waists of the children and clung to them while they wandered around the garden.

She loved playing with them and their toys. She climbed the furniture, the curtains, and the children, sitting on their shoulders to pick through their hair.

She also began to find her voice. At dawn and dusk, she made a whooping noise for her food. She'd start with quiet short whoops and then build on them, making them longer and louder until she was whooping at a thrilling crescendo. *'Whoop whoop whoop! Whoo-oo-oop! Whoo-oo-oo-oo-oo-oop!'*

Zoe and her family woke to this whooping early every morning for the next five years.

Jemima's enclosure was built in the shade of the mango tree. It had a steel frame, a corrugated iron roof, wire mesh walls, and rough cement flooring, and was about the size of a garage. There was a small wooden door big enough for an adult to duck through, and a shelf was tucked high into a corner for Jemima to use as a bed. At one end was the guinea pig enclosure. A second platform in another corner about a meter above the ground served as her meal platform (or her table, as Zoe liked to think of it). A small awning hatch with a bolt and latch on the outside opened outwards from the platform. It was through here that her plate of fruit would be passed through.

'Can I please feed Jemima today?' Zoe asked one weekend.

'Of course you can,' Margie said. 'Can you manage the bolt on the hatch? It can get a bit stuck sometimes.'

'Yes, Mummy. It'll be fine.'

Ibu Marsi had already finished preparing Jemima's supper when Zoe arrived at the

kitchen. 'I'll take her food to her tonight,' Zoe announced proudly. Ibu Marsi smiled at her as she carefully handed her the platter, which was piled high with papaya, banana, mangosteen, and rambutans.

Making Ibu Marsi proud was one of Zoe's main objectives in life. Ibu Marsi had raised the twins their whole lives. Zoe still remembered the feeling of being tied tightly to Ibu Marsi's hip with a sarong as a toddler.

As a Dayak woman from Kalimantan, her ear lobes had been pierced and stretched with metal weights so that they hung low. Zoe had loved to rest her head on Ibu Marsi's shoulder, with her face close to her neck so that she could stroke her earlobes with her forefinger for comfort. She had taught Zoe her first word, 'susu' — 'milk' in Indonesian.

As a smaller child, Ibu Marsi would let Zoe sit on the kitchen bench to watch her grind spices with her stone pestle and mortar, chop vegetables, and prepare meals, teaching Zoe the names of things as she went.

Ibu Marsi always wore her long black hair in a low wide bun pinned into place at the nape of her neck. Zoe would watch fascinated as Ibu Marsi would deftly twist and pin her hair into place.

Ibu Marsi was the first person the children went to when they injured themselves, wrapping bruised legs with papaya leaves, applying obat merah to cuts and grazes, and taking the time to sit quietly with them, wrapped up in her arms, letting their tears wet her blouse, while they breathed in the smell of minyak telon, which she rubbed into their lower back.

Holding the swinging door open for Zoe, she said, '*Hati-hati sayang,*' (Be careful, darling) as Zoe walked slowly through it, balancing the platter between both hands. She kept her eyes on the fruit, willing it not to spill. She could see from where she was walking that Jemima had begun to climb and swing down to the ground in her enclosure. Hooking her fingers through the mesh, she hung there contentedly, kicking

off with her feet, bouncing, chattering, and making short '*ah ah ah*' sounds.

As Zoe approached, Jemima stilled herself and reached one arm through the mesh. She let it hang there casually. Her black eyes watched Zoe closely and then she nonchalantly looked away, as though she wasn't at all excited about being brought her food.

Jemima was fully grown now and was covered with long grey-and-white fur. Her arms were at least twice the length of her body, and she had no tail.

Amused by her nonchalance, Zoe balanced the platter against one hip and reached out to stroke Jemima's long arm. She gently took Jemima's hand and inspected her long, black fingers and perfect fingernails, both so humanlike. 'What a beautiful gibbon you are,' Zoe whispered lovingly, not wanting to break the spell of intimacy.

She normally feared Jemima. Her parents often said, 'Never forget that she's still a wild animal. You must treat her with respect and caution.' And, indeed, as Jemima had grown bigger, she'd developed impossibly long arms and sharp-looking teeth, so it came naturally to treat her with the respect and caution that Margie and Charles instructed the children to act with. But in that moment, Jemima was allowing Zoe to stroke her and come close to her, and Zoe was emboldened by the security of the mesh wire between them.

Suddenly, with a shriek, Jemima grabbed Zoe and pinned her to the fence. She quickly wrapped both arms around her, holding her fast while she bounced her feet wildly off the fence, cackling and shrieking loudly. Terrified by the noise and the proximity of Jemima's teeth to her face, Zoe cried out and struggled to free herself. The platter dropped to the ground, spilling all the fruit across the grass. The tussle only lasted a few moments, but as Zoe landed hard on her bottom, heart pounding, she was equal parts furious and horrified at Jemima's trickery. And to make matters worse, she noticed that in the struggle, she had trodden on some fruit and banana had squashed between her toes. Cross and frightened, Zoe muttered, 'You stupid monkey,' her voice trembling with adrenaline.

Getting on her knees, Zoe collected the fruit, warily keeping her eye on Jemima all the while, who still had an arm hanging through the mesh and her mouth open, teeth bared in a wicked laugh.

When Zoe unlocked the latch to push the platter through the hatch, Jemima climbed up expectantly. Zoe shoved the platter through quickly, terrified Jemima would make a grab for her again, slamming it shut and locking it with relief.

Backing away to a safe distance, Zoe watched Jemima casually start eating. She chose a rambutan first. Once she had popped the delicious pale fruit out of its hairy-looking red skin, she bit into it and pushed it into her mouth. Cheeks bulging, she looked at Zoe innocently and reached for a mangosteen.

Zoe watched for a while, amazed at how much Jemima could fit into her mouth. Jemima barely looked up, engrossed in her meal.

When Zoe tired of watching, she walked back along the driveway, past the pond, and back to the kitchen to find out what was for her own supper.

One Saturday, Pip was heard calling out, 'Mum! Mum! Jemima's broken into the guinea pig cage again!'

When Zoe and Margie reached Pip, who was already in the enclosure, they found Jemima had torn back the chicken wire separating her from the section of the enclosure sealed off for the guinea pigs. She had climbed through, sat herself contentedly in the hay bedding, and caught a guinea pig, which she was now clutching to her chest.

'Quick, Mum! She's holding it too tightly!' Zoe cried.

'Yes, darling, I can see that!' Margie shot back, betraying some panic. 'Let's see if we can get her to put it down gently. Run and get a banana, and we'll try and coax her out.'

When Zoe returned to the cage, she found both Margie and Pip inside Jemima's enclosure, trying to convince Jemima to let go of the guinea pig. Her mother reached for Jemima's hand and tugged it gently, but Jemima bared her teeth — something she always did when she didn't want to give up whatever she was holding. She tucked the guinea pig snugly under her other arm and reached for another. Zoe noticed that the other guinea pig was hiding uselessly in the hay, its head covered but its behind completely exposed. *Daft creature*, Zoe thought, her heart thudding.

'Hand me the banana please, Zoe,' Margie instructed.

Jemima's focus shifted from the guinea pigs to the banana. Pip reached for the limp guinea pig just as Jemima released it and caught it by the leg before it fell onto its head. Concerned, he said, 'It's not moving, Mum.'

Margie, distracted by Jemima (who had climbed onto her hip and was scoffing the banana she'd just been given, munching precipitously close to Margie's face), said, 'Give it a minute. It might come to.'

By now, however, Pip had the guinea pig lying along one arm and was stroking it with the other. 'Come on, little piggie,' he soothed, 'wake up…'

It didn't move.

After some minutes of rubbing, their mother gently said, 'Oh dear. I'm sorry, kids. I think Jemima has loved this one to death as well.'

Zoe felt hot tears well in her eyes. That guinea pig had been one of her favourites. He'd loved to be held and stroked; to be handfed carrots and grass.

With Jemima secured in her enclosure and while new fortifications were being made for the guinea pig cage, the children, in their usual weekend attire of nothing but underpants, crouched over the fresh little grave they'd dug and spelled out 'R.I.P' in twigs. Zoe gathered some flowers, leaves, and stones to decorate it with, and they then held hands, bowed their heads, and said, 'Rest in peace, little piggie.'

The graveyard was starting to take up quite a bit of space in the corner of the garden by the frangipani tree, but they were quickly learning that that was the nature of living with a menagerie of animals.

Several weeks later, the children were dressed and ready for school and eating their breakfast of eggs and toast at the glass-topped wicker table on the patio. Margie watched with consternation as Zoe licked the yolk dribbling down the back of her hand. 'Zoe, please use your knife and fork,' she lectured.

'Yes, Mum. Sorry.' She wiped her hands with her napkin, put it on the table, and picked up her knife and fork.

'And please put your napkin on your lap,' Margie sighed. 'You have better table manners than that.'

Zoe obliged, but the moment her mother's focus was directed back to the newspaper, Zoe picked up her toast with her fingers. Pip mouthed, 'I'm telling on you!' to which Zoe replied by sticking out her tongue.

Suddenly, a cry and a huge splash shattered the morning's calm. Pip and Zoe froze, mouths open, hands in mid-air, holding toast dripping with egg yolk. It took one glance at one another for them to make the silent decision to drop their food onto their plates, scramble from the table, and run to see what had happened. They tore along the patio, ducking through the vine before dashing around the side of the house, through the garden, and towards the swimming pool, in the direction of the noise.

To their surprise, their father was treading water in the middle of the pool, fully clothed in his business suit, still holding his briefcase with one hand, which was now floating beside him. He was wiping water from his eyes, looking shocked.

Jemima was on the edge of the pool cackling, shrieking, whooping, jumping up and down, and swinging her long arms from side to side above her head.

Stunned, Zoe said, 'What happened, Dad? Jemima looks completely crazy! She...' Zoe shook her head in disbelief. 'She looks like she's *laughing*!'

'I think she might be laughing, too,' Charles grumbled, unamused. 'She just pushed me into the pool! I was just taking her back to her enclosure and she suddenly gave me an almighty shove! I lost my balance, and, well...' He tried to shrug, which was harder than it looked in water.

'What on earth!' cried Margie, running onto the scene. 'That monkey!'

'It's alright Margie, I think the joke's on me today,' puffed their dad as he hauled himself out of the pool.

'C'mon, Jemima. I think you've had enough fun,' Pip said, taking Jemima by the hand and walking her to her enclosure.

With a bit more cackling and a backward glance, Jemima happily went with Pip, holding his hand and casually swaying from side to side with each step, her long free arm still in the air.

*

At the weekends, the children loved to hunt for caterpillars.

The best tree to climb was the cassia tree, which shaded the pond, and from her vantage point in its boughs, Zoe looked down at the pond and tried to count the fish. Ringed with white painted stones and filled with pink catfish and bright goldfish, with banks planted with philodendrons and hibiscus, it was a lovely, shady place. It was a glorious day, and the pale green leaves of the cassia tree glowed in the sunlight.

Zoe looked up to see how far Pip had climbed and noticed the dancing coins of brilliant sunlight around her as the breeze gently tossed the branches, and mesmerizingly shifted the light and shade.

'Why aren't you looking for caterpillars?' called Pip from the branches above.

'I am. I'm just resting,' Zoe replied, eyes half-closed.

They were looking for wonderful fat green caterpillars without any stinging hair. They were velvety to touch, and Zoe loved the feeling of their sticky little feet as they crawled along her palm. They had tiny blue dots on their bright green bodies and two false eyes that looked like they had been painted on by hand.

Based on some limited research in the school library, the children surmised that they were tiger swallowtail caterpillars, which would turn into lovely black-and-yellow butterflies. They loved to collect them and keep them in a glass tank, feeding them fresh leaves every day until they started to pupate. And then

they would wait, checking them every day until they hatched into butterflies and could be released into the garden again.

They'd stopped collecting the hairy caterpillars for some time, as they almost always got stung. Zoe remembered the last time this had happened: she'd run to Ibu Marsi, crying as the welts began to redden, rise, and burn. Ibu Marsi had unravelled her bun and brushed the ends of her long hair over the painful stings, explaining that the static this created removed the invisible caterpillar hair from the skin. She'd then calmly walked over to the hibiscus bush and picked a flower. Tearing the petals, filaments, pistils, anthers, and stigma off, she exposed the ovule where a white milk seeped. She gently rubbed this onto the stings, which, as if by some miracle, were almost immediately soothed.

Lost in thought and just as Zoe was picking a leaf with a caterpillar on it to put in her little collecting basket, her mother called from the base of the tree, 'I think Jemima would love to have a climb with you! It's such a lovely day. She has her harness on, so you just need to hang onto the end.'

With that, Jemima reached up to the closest branch and began climbing up to the children.

Pip managed to grab the end of the lead as Jemima swung past him. With a slight tug on the lead, the harness around her waist pulled, forcing her to stop. She sat on the branch near Pip and gradually moved closer to see what he had, picking leaves and twigs and inspecting them before chewing on some and carelessly throwing the less choice ones away.

'I'm just going to sort out lunch. I'll be back in a minute, okay, kids?' Margie called.

'Okay, Mum,' the children shouted down.

Underestimating Jemima's cunning and ambition, Pip let go of the lead to put the caterpillar he'd found in his collector's pouch. Seizing the opportunity, Jemima reached up to the branch above, swung up, and was well out of reach by the time Pip had even realized what had happened.

'Uh oh. Jemima's off,' Pip sighed.

'I'll get Mum,' Zoe called out, climbing down while being careful not to squash her own caterpillar collection. Meanwhile, Pip followed Jemima up the tree, but he was no match for her long arms and fully rotating wrists and shoulders, an evolutionary development that made gibbons especially agile in the jungle canopy. By the time Margie and Zoe returned, Pip and Jemima were high up in the cassia tree on the same bough but just out of reach of one another. Pip grinned and waved.

With her heart in her throat, Margie yelled, 'You are *way* too high, Pip! Come down! Leave Jemima. She'll come down eventually.'

'I'm fine, Mum. I'll catch her.'

Fear and fury painted all over her face, Margie yelled louder, 'Oh no you won't! I said come down, now! No negotiations!'

Reluctantly, Pip began to climb down. dropping to the bough below him. Margie sucked in a breath and held it as she watched, muttering, 'Careful…'

Sighing with relief when Pip was finally on the lowest bough only meters from the ground, Margie set about scolding him when Zoe screamed and pointed in panic. Jemima was soaring through the air with her arms outstretched. Expecting her to fall to her death, they all exclaimed with relief when she instead crashed into the overhanging branch of the trembesi tree growing just outside the garden wall. Shrieking with glee, Jemima scampered up the tree and made a second death-defying leap to the next tree.

Crashing and whooping, Jemima was officially on the loose.

Pip and Zoe yelled for Hariyanto, slipped through the tall black metal gates and ran down the street, calling out, 'Jemima! *Jemima!*'

Hariyanto reluctantly caught up. It was embarrassing enough to be running along the street with two barefoot and barely clothed white kids *without* them yelling out to the damn monkey whooping in the trees. He grinned widely at how absurd it all was.

Up ahead, two men were relaxing on wooden seats under the tree outside their driveway gates, looking curiously at the commotion heading their way. Jemima slowed to a stop above them.

'She's stopped, thank goodness!' Zoe puffed.

'Ten points for guessing why,' Pip said.

The men had been snacking on peanuts and casting the shells to the ground. Jemima eyed them with curiosity.

Zoe called out to the men, *'Maaf bapak, itu adalah monyet kami. Tolong bantu menangkapnya.'* (Sorry sir, that's our monkey. Please help us catch it.)

Nervously, they held the peanuts out so Jemima could see them. She was enticed enough by this to climb down toward them. She paused in the crux of the tree just above their heads and observed them imperiously.

Jogging the last few paces, Hariyanto bent over to catch his breath. His hands on his hips, he managed to reassure the men through his ra-

-gged breath, '*Tidak akan gigit.*' (Won't bite.)

Pip and Zoe finally caught up, puffed their thanks — '*Terima kasih bapak*' — and cooed to Jemima. Hariyanto held the peanuts out to Jemima, who condescended to climb down onto his shoulder and snatch them.

Smiling and shaking his head, Hariyanto promised to come back and pay for the peanuts, as it quickly became apparent that no one was game enough to prise them from her grip.

Relieved, Hariyanto and the children walked back home, laughing every time Hariyanto had to brush the peanut shells that Jemima carelessly dropped out of his hair.

Days later, Margie, Charles, and the children were sitting on the porch facing Jemima's enclosure under the mango tree enjoying vanilla ice cream. Charles had been away for some weeks travelling for work, so the children were regaling their dad with the stories of their adventures, with particular embellishments around Jemima's notorious escape.

'There's the escapee herself!' Charles laughed now, watching Jemima climb down from her bed in the roof of her enclosure. She curled her fingers through the mesh fence and swung from side to side, looking at them expectantly, and rounding her mouth to make her '*ooh ohh*' sounds.

'Looks like she wants to join us,' Margie said, rising to fetch her.

Zoe never tired of seeing Jemima walk in her funny swaying way. She giggled as Jemima stumbled along with one hand in Margie's and the other held above her head.

Once Jemima had loped over to Zoe, she sat in front of her, knees bent into her chest. She rested one long arm on the ground and put her other arm on Zoe's leg, staring at Zoe with that nonchalant gaze before daring a look at the ice cream and inching closer.

'I wonder if she'd like ice cream,' Charles mused. 'She certainly looks interested.'

He offered her his cone. Jemima took it tentatively, licking at the sweet, cool swirl. She licked it again. And then again. Charles tried to take it back, but Jemima bared her teeth and clutched the cone tightly. Laughing, Charles said, 'I guess that's decided, then. No more ice cream for me!'

Zoe was relieved that it wasn't her ice cream that had been sacrificed. She felt compelled to eat hers a little more quickly, lest Jemima should lay claim to hers as well.

Pip laughed out loud, and Zoe grinned at the widening smear of ice cream on Jemima's little face. 'It's dripping off the fur on her chin,' Pip chuckled.

Little did they know that happy moments with Jemima as part of their family were soon to come to an end.

Chapter Three

Pip and Zoe's birthday came around in June of that year. As usual, their mum made one of her wonderful cake creations from her *Women's Weekly* recipe book. This time, the tasty creation was a long green caterpillar: a chocolate cake with whipped green buttercream icing and desiccated coconut as the caterpillar hair. The antennae were little sticks of liquorice, and the eyes were black jellybeans.

Pip was dressed in a white shirt with a frill down the front flaring out either side of the buttons, a purple bowtie, a matching cummerbund, and trousers. Zoe, meanwhile, wore one of her mother's creations: an ankle-length brown gingham dress with an embroidered waistband. The cuff sleeves were also embroidered at the edge, and a white sweetheart collar brightened the whole affair.

As always, neither of them wore any shoes.

At least twenty children had come to the party, and it was a great success. They played pin-the-tail-on-the-donkey, ran three-legged races, bobbed for apples, and played musical chairs and statues and sleeping lions at the end.

As the parents started to arrive to take their children home, the young guests began pressing Margie to keep a promise she had made earlier: 'Please can we pat Jemima? *Please*?'

Margie relented. With the families milling about on the driveway, she went to fetch the little celebrity. As she walked back with Jemima on her hip, Zoe noticed that Jemima looked wary.

The children rushed over to Margie and crowded them both.

'One at a time, please. You're making her

nervous,' Margie said firmly.

The children tried to obey, but were so excited to be patting a gibbon that they jostled and reached over one another, too anxious at the possibility of missing out. Margie could feel Jemima's legs tightening around her and her body stiffening.

'Okay, kids, you *really* need to line up…'

It happened so suddenly that Margie barely had time to react.

Jemima bared her teeth and lunged at the children. In that split second, Margie knew Jemima's intent: she was going to bite one of them. Margie only had one arm around the gibbon and, understanding with panic what Jemima was about to do, she grabbed Jemima's face as it flew towards the children. Protecting the children was Margie's only thought. And, of course, Jemima's sharp teeth sank deeply into the base of her thumb joint.

Margie knew instantly it was a deep bite. Despite the pain that was now searing through her hand, she managed to say through a grimace, 'Sorry, kids. She's too stressed. She has to be put away now.'

Ignoring the moans of disappointment with her teeth gritted, Margie turned away without loosening her grip on Jemima, holding her head to her chest. She felt faint, but managed to get the gate open with her good hand and release Jemima back into her enclosure.

She tucked her injured hand under her armpit and squeezed to staunch the bleeding. She couldn't bring herself to look. Leaning over to lock the latch, she noticed a splodge of blood drop onto the cement floor. Tucking her hand further into her armpit and applying more pressure, she walked unsteadily towards the house when she came across Zoe.

'Darling, this is really important. Go and get me a clean hand towel as quickly as you can,' said Margie with a wobble in her voice.

Immediately noticing how very pale and serious her mother looked, Zoe ran and did as she was bid without question.

'Push the towel against my hand, please,'

Margie said quietly, gingerly lifting her good arm just enough to wedge the towel into her armpit, around her hand.

'Mum, there's so much blood,' Zoe gasped, nauseously taking in the dark stain that was soaking into her silk green shirt.

'Shh, I don't want to worry anyone,' Margie said, managing a small smile. 'Don't say anything. Let's just see off our last guests and I'll get it sorted.'

Uncertain, Zoe did as she was told and joined her parents and her brother to see the last guests off.

'Are you alright, Margie?' one of the mothers asked at one point. 'You look a bit pale.'

'Yes, fine. A small injury. I'll have Charles look at it in a minute. I hope Uma had a nice time?'

'I'm sure she did. Your parties are always the talk of the town!'

Uma grinned, chocolate cake still lodged between her teeth.

Once everyone was waved off, Margie,

feeling faint, turned to Charles and said urgently, 'I think we need to get to the clinic.'

'Let me have a look.' Charles peered under her arm and his face darkened with concern. 'I'll get the car. Kids, go inside.'

With that, he wasted no time in fetching the car keys and his wallet, giving instructions to Marsi to organise supper for the children, oversee their baths, and (never forgetting his manners), to 'please get them to bed'.

Pip and Zoe had traipsed inside as they were told, only to trip each other over in their haste to get to the kitchen window to watch what was happening. On tiptoes and jostling one another to get a better look, they could see their father helping their mother into the passenger seat. She looked unsteady alright.

Jogging around to the driver's seat, Charles had barely climbed in before the car started moving out through the open gates. Pip and Zoe watched until Hariyanto closed the gates and the blinking rear light disappeared from view.

The children didn't see their parents again

before they fell asleep that night. With heavy lids, Zoe said to Pip, 'There was quite a lot of blood. I saw it. I wonder what happened…'

'Me too. Was it Jemima?'

'I don't know, but I think so. Yes.'

When the children came down for breakfast the next morning, the wicker table on the patio was already set and their father was leaning back in his chair and sipping his coffee. He always drank it black. Zoe enjoyed watching him drop a clump of brown sugar into the black liquid and hearing the clink of the spoon against the cup.

Kissing him good morning, she said, 'Is Mummy okay? I saw a lot of blood.'

He wrapped an arm around her, looking uncertain. 'Well, Mummy will be fine. But I need you both to listen carefully now, okay?'

Pip and Zoe nodded gravely and looked at him with wide eyes, fully attentive.

He worked his jaw, his expression distracted. 'She had to have microsurgery on her hand last night. Jemima bit her because she was scared when all the children were crowding around her. We've learnt a very important lesson and been given a very serious reminder: if you remember, we've always said that we must always respect that Jemima is a wild animal, and I think we've become too relaxed with her because she has been part of our family for so long.' The children's eyes were wide. 'What I'm about to say is going to upset you, but you have to listen and try to understand. Your mum and I have been talking, and we don't think it's safe to keep Jemima any longer.'

Shock, cold and numb, seemed to hit both children square in the chest. The first to recover, Pip exclaimed with indignation, 'But Dad, we love her! She's a part of our family! Where would she go?'

'I know. We *all* love her. And we always will. We've been so lucky to have had her in our lives all this time. But yesterday was a serious reminder that all it takes is one bite for her to do irreversible damage. Imagine if she'd bitten one of the children on their faces. Imagine if she bites one of *you* on your faces. You'd be scarred forever, literally.' He wiped his brow with his palm, his eyes fluttering closed momentarily. 'You also have to think about what she needs. Maybe she's lonely. Don't you think she'd like to be with other gibbons? Maybe she'd like to have babies of her own. She's all grown up now, after all.'

'But Daddy, we could get another gibbon for her! We'd make sure to be even more careful,' Pip implored, tears welling in his eyes.

'I'm sorry, my darlings. I know this is hard. Male gibbons can be very aggressive, so it would be too dangerous. The decision has been made. And if you remember, we *had* planned to take her to the rehabilitation centre at the zoo right at the beginning, but they didn't have the space for her. We promised to look after her until they could have her, and as it turns out, she's been with us for much longer than planned because she did so well, and we fell in love with her.' He paused. 'I know there is a primate rehabilitation centre at Ragunan Zoo. A

German lady has dedicated her life to it. I'm sure Jemima will be well looked after. They know how to rehabilitate gibbons for the wild. We must make sure the remaining time we have with her is special.'

Looking forlorn, the children replied, 'Yes, Daddy.'

After that, neither Pip nor Zoe felt much like eating breakfast. Zoe looked out at the garden and watched a green butterfly dance around the bougainvillea.

'It's so unfair. She *belongs* to us,' Pip mumbled under his breath. He looked positively furious.

'I feel so sad.' There was nothing else Zoe felt she could say.

Glancing at the children over the Jakarta Post, Charles said, 'I can see you both look sad about this. Come upstairs and see your mother. She's been resting, but she'll be awake now.'

When they arrived, they found their mother looking sleepy and pale. She was sitting up, leaning on several pillows, and her hand, wrapped thickly in white bandages, was resting on another pile of pillows. Pip and Zoe climbed carefully on her bed, mindful of not knocking her. 'Are you feeling okay, Mummy?' Zoe asked hesitantly.

'Thank you, darling. I'm okay. I feel a little woozy and my whole arm aches, but I'm fine. Daddy makes a good nurse,' she said with a small smile.

'Did you get any stitches?' Pip asked.

'Yes. The surgeon lost count, but I think there are more than twenty in there. Jemima completely lacerated the webbing between my thumb and index finger. I needed microsurgery to reconnect some of the nerves which run along your arm and into the hand, and the thumb tendon needed some repairing, which I now know is called the *flexor pollicis longus*.' She grinned. 'I'm also on antibiotics because animal bites come with a very high risk of infection. There are lots of germs in animal mouths. About as many as there are in human mouths!' She smiled wider at the horrified expressions on the children's faces. The smile faded from her face, however, when she said, 'Has Daddy talked to you about our decision?'

'Yes, Mummy,' Zoe replied despondently.

'Do you understand why she has to be rehomed?'

'Yes,' Pip said quickly, 'but we could be stricter about keeping her in her enclosure.'

'Would that be fair? Gibbons normally have whole jungles to roam in, and they usually live most of their lives in the tops of the trees. At least at a zoo or rehabilitation centre they will have other gibbons to socialise with and much more free space.'

Pip hung his head at his mother's words.

'We've been so lucky to have had Jemima in our lives and to have learned so much, but it's sad that she's not living her life in the jungle as she should be,' Margie said gently. 'I do believe that we gave her a chance at life that she may not have otherwise got because of her damaged foot, but we now know that despite it, she is quite capable. She's been raised on good food, and she's strong. She has a good chance of having a long life now. They can live for up to fifty years.' Her smile returned. 'Normally, silvery Javan gibbons mate for life, so it would be nice if Jemima had the chance to find a mate. They don't have many babies — only one every two to three years, and only one at a time, like people — and as you know, Jemima's mother was killed, and Jemima was kept alive to be sold as a pet. They're endangered. And it would be so nice if Jemima could be a part of the breeding program at one of the zoos or rehab centres so she could contribute to increasing their numbers.' Margie sighed. 'I know it's hard because we love her so much, but it's the right thing to do.'

Defeated and sad, the children nodded. 'We understand,' Zoe said quietly.

'Let's leave Mum to rest now, kids. We'll talk about this again later,' Charles said softly.

The children went downstairs and headed straight to Jemima's enclosure. They leaned against the mesh, and Jemima climbed down to do the same from the other side. Zoe could feel her fur against her skin. She'd stopped grabbing Zoe, and instead, they'd now spend hours sitting like this, leaning against each other and passing each other grass, sticks, and fruit through the holes. Jemima loved to gently pick through Zoe's hair looking for anything edible, and started doing so now.

Zoe was going to miss these moments with her. It felt so nice as Jemima separated her hair bit by bit and gently scratched her scalp.

Zoe gently took hold of one of Jemima's hands. She looked at it closely, wanting to commit every detail to memory. She traced the dark leathery skin of Jemima's palm and her long, narrow fingers — double the length of Zoe's but so human in every other way. Her perfect little fingernails, the creases on the underside of her knuckles... Her thumb, however, was much shorter proportionally than her fingers. Zoe wondered why.

Zoe stroked the long hair on the back of Jemima's hand and up her forearm. It stood on end but wasn't completely straight; it had a tiny crimp to it, and was white at the skin and gradually became grey at the ends.

Zoe felt a deep, hollow sadness settle into her stomach. Both children stayed there until they were called in.

The day of Jemima's departure had arrived.

'We've talked about this. Please don't cry,' Margie said, with tears in her own eyes.

The children watched with dry mouths as Jemima was forced into a small cage. She bared her teeth and shrieked. Pip and Zoe started toward her, but their mother grabbed them and said, 'Stop. It won't make it any easier. It's the right decision. Please be brave.'

Zoe noticed that the tears were now falling freely down her mother's face, and all of a sudden, Zoe couldn't hold her own sobs in. She stole a look at Pip and saw he was crying, too. 'Don't look at me!' he said crossly.

'Alright, kids. It's time,' Charles said delicately, kissing them all and feigning bravery.

Zoe would never forget the sight of Jemima crouched in that too-small cage in the backseat of the Holden Kingswood, her fingers hooked through the top, shrieking with fear. It felt as though she were looking straight at Zoe pleadingly.

Hariyanto closed the passenger door with a clunk of finality. Not being able to see Jemima anymore made panic rise in Zoe's chest. Charles looked at them all furtively and got in the driver's seat of the car. The reflection of the sun on the windows cast the inside of the vehicle in shadow, its tan colour making it fade somehow in the sunlight as it disappeared through the gates. Zoe would always remember that scene in sepia.

They stood there for a moment, the sadness seeping in until Margie bustled them along. It didn't help anyone standing around being mournful.

Jemima's enclosure stood grey and empty, echoing with the years of calling and whooping.

The ghosts of memories drifted around it for weeks. Pip and Zoe missed her deeply. She was gone.

Chapter Four
Several Years Later...

Zoe gazed out at the winter rain. If there was a way to measure raindrops, the ones in Melbourne would score a low two or three for size. Nothing like the tropical drenching rain on the equator!

Feeling homesick, she was anxious to get back to Jakarta for the midyear holidays.

The door to the café opened, admitting a draft of winter chill.

'You're late,' Zoe remarked mildly as her brother, Pip, sat down noisily at the table.

'Yeah. Sorry.'

They were halfway through their second year of university. They'd both stayed on in Melbourne after graduating from boarding school.

'So, all set for the hols?' Zoe asked.

'Yup. You?' Pip was never very generous with words.

'Can Lucy still drive us to the airport?'

Pip nodded.

'Can you keep your goodbyes short? No unnecessary smooching?' Zoe teased.

Pip smirked and leaned back in his chair. His sister hid her smile in her coffee cup as she drained the last of her now-cold café latte. After they'd finalised the details, they sat in amicable silence.

'I wonder what happened to Jemima?' Zoe suddenly wondered aloud.

Pip looked at her and shook his head. 'Not this again. It would be impossible to find her. There's probably zero paperwork to track her. It was years ago that she went to Ragunan Zoo.'

He exhaled. 'Why do you keep bringing this up? You're only setting yourself up for disappointment.'

'Okay. Fine. But just imagine if we did find out what happened to her!' Zoe breathed with that annoying, wide-eyed expression on her face.

'And then what? We find out that she perished from disease at the zoo, or that she was released back into the jungle and met the same fate as her mother? How's that going to make you feel?'

Zoe rolled her eyes. 'I just need to know. That's all. And if I don't find out anything at all, it'll be an adventure, and at least I'll have tried.' She crossed her arms and leaned back in her chair, levelling Pip with a challenging stare.

'Suit yourself, but I think you're a fool for doing it.'

A week later, they arrived at Soekarno Hatta Airport. Zoe loved the way the heat and pungent smells of that metropolis would roll in and envelop them when the airplane door was opened, like a familiar hug.

'Home!' she grinned.

'Yup. You look just as Indonesian as when you last left, sis,' Pip replied sardonically. With their fair skin and generous height, the twins stood out in an Indonesian crowd for sure.

They spent the next few happy days settling in, filling up on nasi goreng and rendang, buying krupuk and Ciklet chewing gum at the pedagang kaki lima on the street corner, and going out to the bars and clubs with their lucky friends who got to stay in Jakarta at the international schools.

It wasn't that boarding was so terrible, and Melbourne was a cool city to live in. Zoe enjoyed the crisp air and the quality of the light; it was brighter somehow. But she had still suffered terribly from homesickness all the way through. Even at the beginning of Year Twelve, she'd cried herself to sleep for the first few nights.

Pip's experience had been worse. He never

talked about it, though. Zoe could only guess at what had happened to him. They had gone to different single-sex schools. If she ever raised it, he'd say it 'wasn't any of her bloody business' and to 'leave it alone'.

It was over supper a few days after arriving in Jakarta that Zoe announced her plan to her parents. 'So, remember Jemima?' she hedged.

'Here we go again,' Charles replied, putting down his knife and fork and reaching for his Bintang Beer.

'Well, I was thinking—'

'She's planning on heading to the jungle to see if she can find Jemima, because apparently after all these years she thinks it would be a good idea,' Pip interrupted with a mouthful of food.

Zoe glared at Pip. 'Thanks a lot!'

'Honey, I know you'd like to find out what happened to Jemima,' Margie said carefully, 'but I think it's a bit of a hopeless quest.'

'Well, I already know how you all feel about this, but I'm going to try,' Zoe responded defensively. 'What I was *going* to tell you is that I'm leaving the day after tomorrow for a week or so.'

'What?' Margie spluttered. 'You can't just… go off into the jungle by yourself!'

'Well, you're welcome to come with me. But just hear me out. Please.'

'Let her speak,' Charles said firmly. 'She's an adult now, after all.' Charles admired an adventurous spirit, and loved it when his kids showed some grit. He'd always challenged them in debate and said, 'Show me your mettle!' if they started to get upset. And, of course, their childhood hadn't been for the fainthearted!

Zoe gave her dad a grateful look and pressed on. 'I went to Ragunan Zoo a couple of days ago, when you thought I'd gone shopping at the mall, and made some inquiries. As it turns out, they had some paperwork about a very tame female gibbon received in 1982 from a western family who'd kept her as a pet, with a distinguishing feature: a damaged left foot.' She grinned as these words sank in and her family's mouths dropped open. 'She was apparently sent to Bandung Zoo in West Java several years ago. They have a rehabilitation program there where they release rehabilitated gibbons into Gunung Gede Pangrango National Park in Bodogol, also in West Java. I thought I could just go for a few days and see what I can find. There's nothing to lose, and at the very least I'll have a bit of an adventure.'

Margie and Charles looked at each other. Margie looked doubtful.

Zoe added, for good measure, 'C'mon, Mum. You backpacked around the world as a twenty-one-year-old! And Dad, you've travelled through these islands for half your life. I'm twenty-one, I speak Indonesian, and I'm sensible.'

Charles considered her words for a moment. 'If it's something you really want to do, then you should go.'

Zoe grinned and squealed, '*Yes!*'

'On one condition.'

Zoe's face dropped.

'Your brother goes with you.'

Pip groaned. '*Nooo*. Do I have to? I was planning on heading to Bali to surf with the guys for a few days!'

'It's only for a few days,' Charles said dismissively. 'You can go to Bali anytime.'

So, it was settled. Their dad usually had the final say, and this occasion was no different.

'I can't believe I've been roped into this,' Pip grumbled.

'Buckle up, bro! It'll be an adventure,' Zoe grinned, unbothered. Nothing was going to wipe the smile off her face. She loved it when she got her own way.

They'd decided to take the train from Gambir Train Station, and were rattling along on the hard seats, backpacks on their laps, windows open, and pressed together by the crowds. Zoe could feel sweat trickling down her back, and could similarly see sweat beading on Pip's top lip. He frowned at her, but she could tell that his lust for adventure was taking over.

He'd be all in on the expedition soon enough.

They arrived in Bandung a few hours later feeling hot and dirty. They caught a battered old Bajaj to their accommodation, a natty little hotel not far from the zoo.

'I think we have time for lunch after we check in and before we're due at the zoo for our appointment at three-thirty,' Zoe said.

'Sounds like a plan. The sooner this is over, the better.'

Zoe rolled her eyes at him.

They found a roadside food stall and devoured their soto ayam and mie goreng. Pip also ordered a Coke.

'That rots your teeth, you know,' Zoe pointed out.

'Whatever.'

Food demolished, they flagged down another Bajaj and headed for the zoo. 'It says here that Bandung Zoo was built in Jubileum Park, a botanical garden created in 1923 to celebrate the Silver Jubilee of Queen Wilhelmina of the Netherlands,' Zoe said, reading from her guidebook. She looked up at the rundown entrance and empty ticket booth. 'It looks like it's seen better days… Hey, could that lady be our contact? They said they'd be standing by the admissions window under the welcome sign.'

'Our names on the carboard sign she's holding are a bit of a giveaway,' Pip responded with a smirk.

'Oh. Yeah. That's helpful,' Zoe said, grinning. She initially hadn't noticed the torn piece of cardboard the lady was holding disinterestedly in her left hand.

Dr Prasetya turned out to be a valuable source of information, and she spoke English well. 'I'm always so excited when westerners show an interest in our conservation programs,' she said. 'It's not just about potential funding, but also about spreading awareness. We have ongoing local education campaigns to try and discourage people from buying primates as pets, and we also try and target the villagers who've found capturing and killing animals to be a good source of income. We are trying to create other sources of income focused more on conservation practices, and to encourage them to understand the value of preserving our forests and natural resources.'

'It must be very rewarding work,' Zoe said, her eyes lit up.

'Most of the time. But it can also be extremely disheartening. We're focused on the long-term aim of preserving and increasing primate populations, which of course involves the preservation of their natural habitat. That is the most challenging aspect of the job, given Indonesia's ever-expanding human population.'

'I'm not sure if the message was passed on from Ragunan Zoo that we had a pet gibbon when we were younger and living in Jakarta,' Zoe said slowly, trying to contain her excitement. 'My parents were against supporting the illegal trade, but because she was injured and looked malnourished, they couldn't help but buy her. They'd planned to take her directly to the zoo, but they had no space for her. So she lived with us for about five years, before she finally went to Ragunan Zoo. We never followed up with them about what happened to her, but I've never forgotten her. So, that's what's started this expedition. We wanted to see what we can find out.'

'Yes, I got the background story,' Dr Prasetya nodded. 'I was really interested, actually, because I remember a female Javan silvery gibbon that came to this centre a few years ago. She was very tame and friendly with zookeepers and staff. I was actually very involved with her; I was part of the team that tried to repair her foot. It was the left one.'

Zoe shot Pip a meaningful look.

'We decided against operating, as she managed well despite it, and it was too late to really do anything about it,' she continued. 'She came with the name Jem. So, there are a few coincidences, but of course no guarantees that it's the same gibbon. But if you're interested, I can take you to where she was released. We sometimes see them, but again, I must repeat, there are no guarantees.'

'That would be great,' Zoe said. 'Even if we don't find her, just to see with my own eyes the forest where she's likely been released will ease my heart.'

So, they made arrangements to leave early the next morning for Bodogol. Dr Prasetya was to collect them from their motel.

'There she is!' Pip said as Dr Prasetya's car drove up to the front of the motel the following morning. Pip and Zoe had been waiting for forty-five minutes.

'*Maaf, jam karet,*' (Sorry, rubber time) Dr. Prasetya said by way of greeting. 'Rubber time' was an Indonesian colloquialism used to excuse tardiness.

After introductions were exchanged between Pip and Zoe and the driver, the twins threw their backpacks into the boot. A few hours later, they arrived at the guesthouse in the national park. They'd spent the journey talking about Jemima and the conservation efforts around Indonesia. They'd settled into lunch at the guesthouse when Dr Prasetya returned with their guide. 'This is Ade. He'll guide us through the forest. We'll camp out tonight on the west side of Mount Gede. I've organised all our supplies.'

Ade was small and wiry. They smiled at one another and exchanged happy greetings.

They set out at around midday, the plan being to set up camp before dark. Gibbons were most active around dawn and dusk, so they wanted to be deep in the forest well before dusk for the best chance of any sightings.

They began their trek along obscured paths under the towering forest canopy. They tripped on the aerial roots of the huge ficus trees and gazed up at the syzygiums and leptospermum javanicums. There were even native magnolias and rhododendrons, which added elegance and colour to the forest. Filling up the forest floor were pandanus trees, vines, and ferns, which formed dense walls of green around them, and the pathway, covered as it was, was often obscured and difficult to follow.

'Did you hear that?' Dr Prasetya said suddenly.

Pip and Zoe stopped and strained to hear. Zoe felt herself holding her breath. There was a distinct whooping call in the distance.

Zoe snatched her binoculars and raked the canopy to see if she could make anything out.

'They'll just be getting warmed up. We're not far from camp, so let's keep going,' Dr Prasetya suggested quietly.

Their camp was a small clearing on the forest floor. Small footpaths had been cleared through the forest. 'The girls' toilet is that way, and the boys' toilet is that way,' Dr Prasetya said, pointing to two paths going in opposite directions from the campsite and into the forest. A spade had been driven into the ground and stood like a sentry at the beginning of each. A third pathway led to a timber lookout that stood several feet above the forest floor, and approximately ten meters away from that was a second timber platform sitting on top of four poles. 'You see that timber platform there?' Dr Prasetya asked, following Pip and Zoe's gaze. 'We leave fruit and food that the primates like and then observe them from our platform. When we're preparing to release them, we start by keeping them captive but feeding them for a few days. Then, when they're released, they understand that they can rely on a food supply here while they adapt to their new surroundings. Over time, their visits become rarer and rarer.'

Right on cue, Ade took a box of fruit that he'd carried into the forest, climbed up the side of the timber frame, and emptied the fruit on top of the platform. He was agile and quick; he'd obviously done this many times before.

He returned to the lookout, Pip and Zoe shuffling over to make room for him.

'I'm starving!' Pip said as Ade passed them all their supper of nasi bungkus. They opened their parcels wrapped in banana leaf and hungrily ate the cold steamed rice, fried chicken, diced green beans, chili, and golden, greasy, deep-fried boiled egg.

They talked quietly while they ate and waited.

Darkness descended quickly in the forest, and it didn't take long for Zoe to start feeling a little spooked.

'We've been unlucky tonight,' Dr Prasetya finally sighed. 'Let's turn in and we'll come back before first light.'

They stumbled and fumbled their way back to the campsite. It seemed much further away than it had earlier. They were all grateful for their torches, which they kept focused on the ground for fear of pythons.

'Well, that was disappointing,' Pip said pointedly once they were back, rummaging for their toothbrushes and pyjamas. 'I hope you're preparing yourself for the possibility of not seeing anything of interest at all, Zoe.'

'I know. But as I said to you and Mum and Dad, at least I will have tried. That'll have to be good enough.' She paused, suddenly frowning.

'Unless we stay for a week…?'

Pip slapped at another mosquito. 'Not on your life.'

Chapter Five

'Mr Pip. Miss Zoe.'

Silence.

'Mr Pip! Miss Zoe!'

Zoe was in a deep, heavy sleep even though she was actually very uncomfortable on the forest floor, her sleeping mat no match for the twigs beneath, which were digging into her back.

'Mr Pip. Miss Zoe!'

Zoe felt a jab in her shoulder.

'Wake up, sis. This is what you wanted,' Pip's voice grumbled blearily. 'Thanks, Ade. We're awake.'

Zoe groaned. She'd never been a morning person.

The twins pulled on their trousers, boots, and jackets. It was surprisingly cold in the forest. Headtorches on, they scrambled out of their tents to join Ade and Dr Prasetya. In single file and complete silence, they made their way back to the lookout. Thankfully, Ade produced a thermos filled with hot sweet black Indonesian coffee, bananas, cold boiled eggs, and some stale sweet bread to wake them up with, which lifted everyone's mood.

The darkness started to almost imperceptibly change to grey as dawn approached. The sounds of the forest had been building in that predawn darkness, and the cacophony was suddenly almost deafening. One sound in particular pierced distinctly through the din. Pip and Zoe looked at each other, eyes wide. They had both heard it. It was a sound they'd recognize anywhere.

The dawn whooping call of the Javan silvery gibbon.

Binoculars at the ready, they raked the canopy again and again. Ade tapped them both on their arm to get their attention, pointing at something with a grin. Pip and Zoe retrained their binoculars on the shape in the distance, half concealed in the canopy.

As if sensing their presence, it turned and looked at them. It was definitely a gibbon.

Zoe grinned.

They all watched as that single gibbon turned into a family of five: two parents, two adolescents, and one baby clinging to its mother. Whooping and calling, they swung through the canopy and climbed lower and lower through the branches.

'These are definitely rehabilitated gibbons,' Dr Prasetya whispered. 'They've seen us, but they're not afraid to approach, and they know we've brought them food.'

Pip and Zoe kept their binoculars trained on the gibbons. They didn't need to say anything to know they were both looking for the same thing. They wanted to get a proper view of the mother's left foot.

It was hard to make out; the gibbons moved so quickly. Before long, they were all on the timber platform helping themselves to the fruit left there. Ade had added more that morning knowing that half would disappear overnight, as there were other hungry forest creatures scavenging for food.

The mother climbed up into a nearby bough, and there... there it was. Her foot. Still damaged, still twisted, but not holding her back.

Zoe gasped and elbowed her brother hard in the ribs. Pip mouthed, 'Ow!' but his face was filled with elation. Zoe knew he could barely believe it, even though he had privately harboured the same hope that she had. Tears of happiness sprung to Zoe's eyes as they watched Jemima with her family.

'Is it okay if I call her name?' Zoe asked after some time of awe-struck silence. 'I know it's been a long time, but... I'm curious. Will it frighten them?'

'They're used to us,' Dr Prasetya assured

her. 'See what happens.'

'Jemima!' Zoe called. 'Jemima!'

The gibbon stopped eating her fruit mid-chew. She looked over at the lookout.

Pip and Zoe froze.

Pip joined in. 'Jemima! Jemima!'

'It's definitely her. I can't believe it,' Zoe breathed. 'Look, she's coming closer!'

'Hello, Jemima!' Pip cooed, in awe. 'Are these your babies?'

They kept talking gently as Jemima came closer still. She stopped a few meters away on a low branch. The baby turned its head to look at them. It had no fur except for a little tuft on its head, and was clearly still suckling. Jemima watched them for a while, listening to Pip and Zoe talk to her and call her name. Then, she climbed down the tree and swung over to the closest branch to the lookout. She was two meters away from Pip and Zoe.

'Come and show me your baby, Jemima. Come,' Zoe whispered. She was barely breathing.

Dr Prasetya took out her handheld camera and started filming. 'This is so lovely,' she murmured.

Jemima reached out to the timber railing of the lookout and sat there looking at them for a minute, as if to contemplate what to do. The jungle wilds had made her wary.

Zoe reached out her hand. Jemima hesitated but then took it and climbed onto Zoe's shoulder. Zoe's face was inches away from the baby. She could barely believe it. 'Jemima, do you remember us?'

As if in answer, Jemima climbed down onto the lookout floor to sit between Pip and Zoe. She rested one hand on Pip's leg and the other on Zoe's arm. They both stroked her and smiled. All the while, the baby clung to its mother, turning its little head one way and then the other, and gazing at them as if to assess them.

'Isn't she divine,' Zoe laughed between tears.

'Pretty gorgeous,' Pip murmured, looking very moved himself.

Ade and Dr Prasetya looked utterly joyful. While the aim of the rehabilitation program was to reduce human contact with primates, this was an exception to the rule. It was incredibly touching to witness.

Suddenly, there was a whoop from above. They all looked up to find a male gibbon calling to Jemima and the adolescents, swinging from branch to branch.

Jemima looked at Zoe and then at Pip, holding their gaze. She then climbed into Zoe's lap and sat there for a moment. Zoe put her arm around Jemima and, hesitatingly, stroked the back of the baby's head with her forefinger. She worried that Jemima would react with panic or aggression, but she didn't. She rounded her mouth and made a quiet '*ooh, ooh*' noise. The baby closed its eyes and leaned into Jemima's chest contentedly.

Eyes wide, Pip reached over to stroke the baby, too. Jemima watched patiently and happily, as though she were proud to share her joy.

The male gibbon called again. Jemima looked at him and made that soft *'ooh, ooh'* noise again as though to convey that she had to go soon. She sat there for a moment, turning to look at Pip and Zoe.

'It's okay, Jemima,' Zoe urged. 'Go to your family. I'm so happy to see you where you should have always been.'

As if acknowledging this, Jemima held Zoe's gaze, made another noise, climbed onto the railing, grabbed the branch of the tree, and climbed away. Pip, Zoe, Ade, and Dr Prasetya watched as Jemima and her baby joined their family. With one final backward glance, the gibbons swung out of sight.

The group sat in silence for a while as they processed what had happened. They all knew it was special. Very special.

'Well, you got your wish,' Pip smiled.

'I did indeed,' said Zoe as she leaned back on the railing. She wiped a tear away with the palm of her hand. 'She is where she's meant to be.'

Acknowledgements

I would like to thank Emmie Press for making the publication of *Pip and Zoe's Amazing Adventures* possible. I would never have followed through without Hayley and Elise's gentle encouragement and support. Thank you for your extraordinary patience as life events set back the finish line several times. I am deeply grateful.

It goes without saying that I am unbelievably grateful to the universe for delivering Cassia Whitton, illustrator extraordinaire, to me. For someone who started out as my neighbour's girlfriend's friend's daughter, thank you so much for agreeing to illustrate this collection of stories. You have brought to life my childhood with incredible precision, patience, and grace. I am still completely bewildered over how you can turn the stick figures, squiggles, and verbose descriptions of my childhood memories into exquisite illustrations. I am also so honoured to be a part of the beginning of your career as an artist. There is no doubt you will go far. Please don't disappear! I'm hoping we can bring more of *Pip and Zoe's Amazing Adventures* to life together.

To Jo Whitton of Quirky Cooking (Cassia's mother): thank you for encouraging Cassia to take the plunge with me and for the encouragement and guidance you continue to give us both.

To Indonesia: for your chaos and beauty, thank you for giving me what I now understand to be an extraordinary childhood. This is a lifelong love affair.

To my dad, Tim Cottew, without whom this book would never have come into being. I thank you from the bottom of my heart for backing me financially and emotionally through not only the process of writing these stories, but also through a period of wild tumult in my life. My deepest gratitude and thanks. I love you. But more importantly, thank you for being the eccentric, adventurous soul that you are; for showing me the world and pushing me to be brave enough to take risks, seek, and explore. Who on earth would I be without you?

To my big brother, Piers (Pip), with whom I got up to plenty of mischief as a child. I swear it was you who led me astray! Thank you for letting me tell our stories. I think I have kept the promise I made when you gave me your permission to tell our tales and you said, 'So long as you don't make me look like an idiot.' I love you, bro.

To my siblings, Dani and Rory, for your love and support throughout. You are my best friends. I promise there will be novels dedicated to you both in the future. I love you both, too.

To my mum, Helen, for your relentless and staunch support throughout my life. Thank you. Another adventurer and eccentric… I mean, really, what hope did any of us children have? No wonder none of us have gone down the beaten path! But most of all, thank you for taking me, my children, and our dog in at a chaotic time in our lives. We will be forever grateful. Your care and support have made it possible for me to dedicate the necessary time to this project. So much love to you.

To my children, Astrid, Archie, and Niamh, you are my whole world. Thank you for asking for 'stories from your mouth' when you were toddlers, which started this whole thing. I loved telling you stories about my childhood in Indonesia, which inspired giggles, wide eyes, and complaints that you couldn't have a pet gibbon, too.

Mandy Lade: I will be forever grateful for the fact that when I explained to you, the nicest prep teacher you could ever ask for, what 'stories from your mouth' meant (in case my daughter suggested you do the same), you said that 'they sound like a lovely collection of children's stories' — which planted the seed almost a decade ago! Thank you.

To our goldendoodle, Spencer, for being the

best dog in with world. He is the best coparent I could ever ask for, and the best footrest! He spent hours curled up under my desk and around my feet as I wrote these stories.

To my friends, the bestest of the best, for always telling me to press on when I felt I couldn't take another step. A heartfelt thank you.

About the Author

Zoe Cottew's childhood in 'seventies and 'eighties Indonesia inspired her debut collection of short stories for children, *Pip and Zoe's Amazing Adventures.*

Growing up with a menagerie of animals, including Jemima the Gibbon, exploring the Thousand Islands in the Java Sea, making fairy gardens in the tea plantations, and digging heffalump traps in the sands of Carita Beach, inspired a lifetime of travel and adventure for Zoe and her daring older brother, Pip.

During the course of her life so far, Zoe has lived in Indonesia, England, France, East Timor, Jordan, and Australia. When she's not drifting between the wild world of her own imagination and reality, she's adjudicating over whose turn it is to feed the dogs and put the chickens away.

Zoe, her three gorgeous children, and their goldendoodle, Spencer, currently live with Nana Helen, Uncle Rory, and Windy Indie the giant poodle, in a stone house in the woods in the beautiful Macedon Ranges, Victoria, Australia.

www.pipandzoesamazingadventures.com
www.instagram.com/pipandzoes_amazingadventures

About the Illustrator

Cassia Whitton is a young artist who lives on the Atherton Tablelands in Far North Queensland. Educated at home, her love for art, nature, and creativity was nurtured by her mother from a young age. Cassia specialises in watercolours and has mastered the art of bringing animals to life with her brush.

In 2020, at seventeen years old, Cassia's commissioned pet portraits began touching the lives of families who cherished their beloved animals, and in 2022, she embarked on the exciting path of illustrating Zoe Cottew's *Pip and Zoe's Amazing Adventures*. Now a full-time artist, Cassia aspires to bridge the gap between words and visuals, evoking emotions and sparking imaginations.

Appendix

(The Real) Baby Zoe and Jemima

For more wonderful photographs, please visit
www.instagram.com/pipandzoes_amazingadventures
or www.pipandzoesamazingadventures.com.